Brad Hauck

I0037027

RUN
TOWARDS
THE
FLAMES

Mastering Leadership in Times of Crisis

iX
IndieXperts
PUBLISHING & AUTHOR SERVICES

First published 2024 by Brad Hauck

Published by Brad Hauck

Produced by Indie Experts
indieexperts.com.au

Cover design and typesetting by
Ammie Christiansen, Fast Forward Design
Typeset in 11pt Minion Pro

ISBN
Printed: 978-1-7636051-3-8
eBook: 978-1-7636051-2-1

Disclaimer:

Every effort has been made to ensure this book is as accurate and complete as possible, however they may be errors both typographical and in content. The author and the publisher shall not be held liable or responsible to any person or entity with respect to any loss or damage caused or alleged to have been caused directly or indirectly by the information contained in this book.

Some names and identifying details in this book have been changed to protect the privacy of individuals.

Dedication

*To my wife and my children, who have walked every step
of this journey with me, believing in me when I didn't,
strengthening me and helping me to become who I am.*

Contents

Introduction

Hi, I'm Brad Hauck, and over the past 20 years my journey has been profoundly shaped by two influences: my passion for firefighting and my experiences as an entrepreneur. As I was growing up, the tales of bravery and sacrifice my Godfather, a dedicated firefighter, would share instilled in me a deep respect for this demanding profession. He taught me that firefighting was not just about battling flames but about living with purpose and readiness, knowing full well that each call could be your last. This perspective led me to become a volunteer firefighter in my thirties, balancing my professional life with the commitment to serve my community.

My involvement in firefighting, particularly in fighting and managing wildland fires, has honed skills which have proven invaluable in the business world. These are not your typical building fires that can be surrounded and subdued; these are wildfires that require strategic thinking, coordination across large teams, and enduring tactics, often stretching over weeks. Each fire is an exercise in leadership, demanding clear strategy implementation and adaptive problem-solving under pressure in rapidly changing environments.

Throughout my firefighting career, I've worked alongside a diverse array of leaders—surgeons, lawyers, tradespeople, and more—each bringing their unique perspectives to leadership. This experience has enriched my understanding of effective people management in business endeavours. Whether leading a team through the unpredictable dynamics of digital marketing or steering a project to success against tight deadlines, the adaptability, resilience, and tactical acuity learnt on the fireground have been my guide.

In this book, I aim to bridge the divergent worlds of firefighting and business leadership. The lessons learned in the heat of battle against nature's fury are lessons in agile leadership, strategy, and resilience. They taught me about adapting to change, of being prepared for any contingency, and of leading with courage and decisiveness. Whether you're facing an unpredictable marketplace or the fires of the Australian bush, the principles of leadership remain the same.

Join me as we explore how the disciplines of firefighting can inform and transform business leadership, turning you into a leader who is not only prepared to face changes but is also equipped to thrive amidst them. Here's to learning how to win, no matter what challenges we face, because in both firefighting and business, there is no room for second best. We either win or we win. There is no other option when the world around you is on fire!

Change is Inevitable

"Change is inevitable: Fan its flames to forge new paths, not just extinguish old ones."

Chapter 1:

Embracing the Inevitability of Change

Change is a constant force in our lives, shaping our experiences, testing our resilience, and stretching the boundaries of our comfort zones. This chapter explores the importance of accepting and adapting to change, both in the volatile environment of firefighting and in the dynamic world of leadership and business because no matter what you do to fight it, change will happen.

As a firefighter, I've come to understand that change is a part of every call and operation. We don't wait to see if things will change; we prepare for when they will. This is also true in the world of digital marketing. A proactive mindset is crucial not only on the fireground but also in navigating the challenges you'll face in everyday life and business.

I have learned to appreciate change because it forces me to grow stronger, become more flexible, and develop resilience in the face of adversity. However, embracing change does not come naturally to everyone. Like many, I find comfort in routine. Yet I am also driven by the desire for improvement, which inevitably requires adapting to new circumstances, and that isn't always fun.

In leadership, the ability to pivot, to make decisive choices in the face of shifting conditions, is a vital skill. Whether it involves making small adjustments or undertaking significant transformations, how we manage change can define our success or failure. The obstacles we face might seem insurmountable, but breaking through these barriers propels us forward more effectively than following the easy path ever could.

Throughout this chapter, we will explore strategies for dealing with change, not just surviving but thriving in its wake. By building a supportive team and leveraging collective knowledge and experience, leaders can enhance their ability to navigate change. True leadership is about making progress through the unpredictable, using every twist and turn as an opportunity to learn and evolve.

Together, we'll discover why facing change head on is essential for growth, and why the ability to adapt is one of the most powerful tools at our disposal.

It's not what happens, it's how you deal with it that counts!

The morning air was tense with the stillness that comes before a battle. As the vast bushfire slowly crept toward us, its massive presence loomed like a silent giant. Despite its slow advance, we knew better than to underestimate its potential. We were used to "hurry up and wait". It meant that we needed to be ready, but it could be some time until we needed to go into action.

We took advantage of the deceptive calm, setting up a cricket game to lighten the mood. The crack of the bat and laughter briefly cut through the smoky haze, a momentary respite from the looming threat.

"All right, team, take a break!" the Sector Commander called out as everyone was gathered around, enjoying the game. The crews cheered for one last hit before we shifted our focus back to the job at hand.

While we played, bulldozers worked diligently nearby, carving a long containment line parallel to the fire's flank. This line was our main line of defence, a barrier we hoped would hold the fire at bay.

Suddenly, the radio crackled to life, startling us into silence. "Shift in the wind direction, 90 degrees—urgent update required," the Ops Officer announced, her voice cutting sharply through the light-hearted atmosphere.

The game stopped abruptly. The Sector Commander grabbed the radio, pressing the receiver tightly. "Copy that. Can you confirm the fire is heading directly towards us now?" he asked, as a knot formed in my stomach.

"Affirmative," came the reply. "The flank has shifted. You've got about 7 kilometres of fire heading straight for your position. We need you to put in a backburn along that dozer line immediately to contain it."

The news hit us hard. The cricket bat dropped to the ground with a thud as reality sank in. Our brief diversion was over; it was time to get serious.

"Pack it up, boys," the Sector Commander said firmly, gesturing towards the trucks. "We've got work to do."

We moved quickly, the earlier calm replaced by a flurry of activity as we donned helmets, jackets and gloves. The bulldozer track, once a mere precaution, had suddenly become crucial.

As we drove to the end of the dozer line, we were briefed. "Listen up! We're going to start backburning from this point. Keep it tight and watch for spot fires. This burn needs to be clean—we can't afford any slip-ups."

The trucks spread out, stationed 300 meters apart along the line. The heat was oppressive, the air shimmering above the ground as the temperature soared to 40 degrees Celsius. Sweat dripped into my eyes as I lit the drip torch, the flame tiny yet fierce against the vastness of the bush.

"Fire on the ground! Keep an eye on the spread," I called over the radio as the roar of the flames and the underbrush crackled.

For the next ten hours, we fought tirelessly. The line of fire we created consumed the undergrowth, eating away at the fuel in the path of the oncoming blaze. Every firefighter was focused, their faces set in grim determination as they managed their sections of the burn.

Finally, long after the sun dipped below the horizon, we completed our task. The backburn had held, and the flank of the fire was contained within the boundaries we had set.

Exhausted but satisfied, the Sector Commander radioed in our status. "Containment line is secure. The fire's held."

As we regrouped and headed off the fireground, the relief was palpable, our exhaustion eclipsed by the pride of a job well done.

In the world of firefighting, as in life, expecting the unexpected and having a plan in place had made all the difference. Today, it had turned what could have been a disaster into a testament to our preparedness and resolve.

Firefighting is an unpredictable profession. Each call brings a unique set of challenges, often vastly different from what was anticipated. This dynamic environment has shaped me not only as a firefighter but also as an entrepreneur, where the business landscape is similarly fluid and ever-shifting.

In the volatile world of business, change tests our resilience and pushes the boundaries of our comfort zones. As a business leader, you must embrace the inevitability of change, much like the firefighters.

You must adopt a proactive mindset and prepare for when change will occur, rather than waiting to see if it will. Whether it's navigating an evolving digital landscape or responding to shifting market conditions, the ability to make decisive choices in the face of change is vital.

Successful business leaders understand that true leadership is about making progress through the unpredictable, using every twist and turn as an opportunity to gain experience and evolve. If you can embrace change, adapt to new circumstances, and find opportunities in the face of adversity, you will be the one who will lead your organisation to greater success—just as firefighters recognise that "it's how we respond that counts".

Responding to Change

The life of a firefighter involves constant vigilance—monitoring weather, terrain, and fire behaviour to anticipate and react to changes. This mindset is equally applicable in the business world, where client demands, technological/market advancements, and competitors' actions are in perpetual flux.

In both arenas, preparation and training are key. Firefighting drills, often based on scenario planning, equip teams with the mental and physical flexibility to handle various emergencies. These exercises develop a mindset that is critical for business leaders: the ability to pivot strategy at a moment's notice.

For example, during fire season, we meticulously analyse forward weather reports and fire behaviour predictions to prepare for potential outbreaks. Similarly, in business, leaders must stay informed about industry trends and shifts in consumer behaviour to anticipate changes that could impact their operations.

This was evident during the COVID-19 pandemic, where businesses that had cultivated agility and a readiness to adapt were better positioned to navigate the crisis. Like firefighters who must adapt to the wind's shift, companies had to pivot quickly, whether by adopting new technologies like Zoom or modifying their business models.

To foster this resilience, businesses can adopt practices from fire-fighting, such as regular scenario-based training and strategic planning sessions that encourage quick thinking and problem-solving. Just as firefighters debrief after an incident to learn from their experiences, businesses should also analyse their performance during and after crises to improve their responses to future challenges. Learn what worked and discard what didn't, so next time you can react more efficiently.

By expecting it, preparing for it, and learning from each encounter, you can harness change as an opportunity for growth and innovation.

Recently, I participated in combating a significant bushfire in Australia. It had been ravaging the local area for days before our team was deployed to assist the local crews. The long journey to the fire gave us ample time to strategize; yet upon arrival, the scenario was drastically different from our expectations. The fire was advancing through bushland spotted with natural gas wells, unpredictably close to crossing the road into an adjacent area, which could have led to catastrophic spread.

Our task was straightforward in theory but complex in execution: keep the fire contained on one side of the road without letting it jump across. We positioned our five trucks strategically along the road, spacing them out to cover the area. I was assigned to a light attack unit, ready to address any embers that might breach our line.

Initially, the situation seemed under control. The fire behaved as expected, moving predictively within the bush at a low level and not posing immediate threats to the road. However, the wind shifted unexpectedly, bringing smoke, flames and embers towards the road, complicating our operation. This change was quick, rapidly transforming the fire's behaviour and increasing the potential for a burnover—a deadly scenario where flames overtake firefighters, who have no chance for escape.

Our teams' communication became crucial as the situation evolved.

We adapted quickly, responding to new spot fires caused by flying embers with precision. Despite our efforts, the wind intensified, pushing the fire up from the ground and flaming out of the treetops, creating a new front that was terrifying in scale and intensity.

The climax of our battle came when a fire bomber delivered a timely drop of water and foam, quenching the flames and giving us a momentary reprieve. This allowed us to regroup and address the resurgence of embers, which had begun to fall with increasing frequency. Just as we thought we might regain control, the fire's magnitude once again increased, forcing us to reconsider our strategy. We decided to withdraw, prioritising the safety of our team and preparing for structural defence to protect the local community.

This experience underlines a critical lesson: conditions can change with alarming speed, and success depends on our ability to anticipate and react without hesitation. One minute, everything can be calm and normal; next minute, you have an uncontrollable wildfire on your hands!

Overcoming the Fear of Change

Fear is an innate response to potential danger, but in any situation, it is not an excuse for inaction. Instead, it should be a powerful motivator for preparation and rapid response. A well-trained firefighter understands that fear is a part of the job, but this awareness drives them to perform with precision rather than panic. The best firefighters are calm under pressure. This principle applies equally to business, where you need to navigate uncertainty with foresight and agility.

During a massive wildfire, the conditions on the ground can shift unpredictably. For instance, while managing a large bushfire, we faced an unexpected change when the fire jumped a containment line despite our thorough preparations. This scenario mirrors business situations where, despite rigorous planning, external factors like market shifts or technological disruptions cause chaos when they shatter your best-laid plans.

In both contexts, maintaining composure and focusing on well-rehearsed procedures helps manage the situation. In firefighting, this might mean executing a planned backburn; in business, it might involve activating a contingency plan or innovating under pressure. The key is to stay informed and prepared, making fear a catalyst for action rather than a paralysing force.

It had been a pretty normal week in the office, working on client websites to improve their search engine rankings and dealing with the usual technical difficulties that happen with websites. The mood was positive, and we were seeing the results we wanted. Then, an email arrived in my inbox from Google, informing me of new algorithm changes. It didn't specify the exact changes but explained the goal was to enhance search results for users. In the SEO world, this meant we were about to see some movement in all our clients' rankings.

Many of our clients had top 10 rankings on Google, so we anticipated some fluctuation in their rankings until things settled down. We were confident in our "white hat" SEO practices and expected the rankings to return to their original positions once the updates fully rolled out. However, we had no control over how long this process would take. White hat SEO improves a website's search ranking by following search engine rules. It's the opposite of black hat SEO, which cheats the system to get higher rankings. To ensure everyone was aware of the change, I sent out an email explaining the update and what people could expect.

Three days later, I received an irate call from one of our clients. They were demanding immediate action because their site had dropped off the first page of search results. I could hear the fear in their voice. When I asked if they had read the email I sent, they confirmed they had but pointed out that their phones had stopped ringing and no clients were calling about their services. They blamed me because they paid us to keep them at the top of the rankings, and without new business, they wouldn't be able to keep their doors open.

Initially, I was quite upset. As a leader, I take the success of my clients personally. I knew there was nothing I could do to speed up the algorithm's adjustment period, but that didn't make the situation any easier. Then, I had a thought. I asked them, "What are you seeing from your other advertising?" Personally, I had a range of lead generating advertising as being a firefighter, I understood I couldn't rely on my results always staying the same. Something always changes and I want to protect my business.

Their answer hit me like a baseball bat between the eyes. "I don't do any other advertising." Despite our discussions about the volatility of Google rankings and the importance of diversifying their marketing efforts, they had taken no steps to protect their business in advance. They were blaming me for their failure to diversify! After answering my question, they must have realised the same thing. They apologised, thanked me for my work, and hung up. Four days later, their rankings bounced back to #1 on Google. Talking to them later, I discovered they had increased their efforts to get leads outside of their website.

Fear makes people do irrational things. Just like firefighters expect things to change, you being prepared in advance ensures your business doesn't collapse at the first signs of major change.

Embracing and Leading through Change

Firefighters are trained to handle sudden shifts in fire behaviour, changes in orders, and moving from offensive to defensive strategies in an instant. This readiness for change is critical for you as well. Leaders who embrace change rather than resist it can navigate their teams through uncertainties more effectively.

The concept of "running towards the flames" epitomises the initiative-taking mindset I encourage leaders to take. In firefighting, this means addressing the fire aggressively before it grows into an uncontrollable monster. Small fires left alone to burn quickly turn into large fires. In business, it translates into attacking challenges and changes before they turn into big problems. You should see them as opportunities for growth and innovation. Leaders who cultivate this mindset can build resilient teams capable of thriving in dynamic conditions.

Both fields require a culture of continuous learning through planned scenarios. Regular training and simulations in firefighting prepare teams for various emergencies; in business, regular strategic reviews and skills development sessions achieve the same effect. Additionally, creating a playbook for emergency procedures in business, akin to a firefighter's Field Incident Guide (FIG), can provide a valuable "go to" resource during crises. The FIG is a comprehensive collection of information to help firefighters make decisions. It contains the "how to" of everything from aircraft management to wind strength measurement.

The principles of leadership in firefighting—preparedness, rapid response to change, and the effective management of fear—are equally applicable in your business. By adopting these practices, you can foster resilience and adaptability in your teams, equipping them to meet any challenge with confidence and strategic foresight.

Facing Fear in Leadership

As we approached the sprawling fireground, the thick, acrid smoke obscured our vision, rendering the open country ahead almost invisible. The radio crackled to life, breaking the tense silence inside our truck.

"Looks like we're flying blind," I muttered, my eyes scanning the dense smoke. "Keep your head on a swivel. We don't know what we're driving into."

"Roger that," came a reply from the back. The chatter among the crew had died down as the gravity of the situation settled in. We were about to enter a battlefield where the enemy was unpredictable and ever-changing.

We arrived at the Divisional Command point to meet up with the local crews. A quick briefing revealed the massive task ahead: our division spanned over 30 kilometres, and we had only seven trucks to cover it.

"Seven trucks for 38 kilometres ? That's stretching it thin," one of the crew members voiced, echoing the concern in all our minds.

As we began our initial assessment, a call came in from the Helitaks (firefighting helicopters) overhead. "Helitak 412 to Alpha Sector, we've spotted a large smoke plume at the end of your track. Looks like the fire might have jumped the road south of your position. Investigating..."

The tension in the truck ramped up. "I need a crew to head out and check it," the Div Comm called. We dispatched two trucks to the reported location. The feedback was grim. The fire had indeed crossed over, burning a swath about 600 metres wide, over 100 metres into the bush from our main track.

"This changes everything," I said to the team. "We'll soon need to fall back to work on that containment line we've just driven. Better get ready to move."

While we waited, we organised a backburn to attempt to secure the fire to the original side of the road. The original fire front was still burning towards us, threatening to jump the containment line we were currently watching. Suddenly the wind began to pick up, carrying a new wave of anxiety with it. The radio chatter became more urgent.

"Wind's shifting! It's picking up speed!" one of the lookouts alerted.

I grabbed the radio. "All units, stay alert. We're going to try to put in this backburn, but we may need to move if things keep changing. Keep your ears open in case we need to pull out."

The crews worked feverishly to burn the fuel and create a barrier. But nature was faster. Ten minutes later, the wind had turned hostile, propelling the fire towards us with terrifying speed. It was now leaping out of the tops of the trees, dropping embers onto the unburnt side. A monstrous wave of flames was quicky bearing down on us.

"All crews pull out to Div Com. We've got to go now!" ordered the Strike Team Leader over the radio.

"Copy that. Everyone, pack up and get in your trucks!" I replied. As I headed to my truck, I noticed two crews further down the track, out of radio contact. My heart raced as I walked towards them, the heat pressing against my face like an open oven.

"Move out now! It's coming over!" I shouted over the noise of the pumps as I reached them. The urgency in my voice spurred everyone into action. We were a team, and no one would be left behind.

Back at the truck, embers danced around us like fiery snowflakes, each one a potential disaster. Spot fires erupted on the roadside, a stark reminder of our precarious situation.

Yet, amid the chaos, I felt a surge of adrenaline, not fear. It was exhilarating, in a way, to be at the heart of such raw power. But more than that, I knew my role was to remain composed—for my crews, for the operation, for everyone relying on us to hold the line.

"Let's get out of here," I said to my crew, a determined grin spreading across my face despite the looming danger. "Keep focussed, and keep moving forward safely."

As we manoeuvred out of harm's way, the fire raged around us. In that moment, leading my crew to safety, the significance of our work had never been clearer. When the world is on fire around you, fear has no place. You face the inferno, you adapt, and you overcome.

Turning fear into preparedness is essential for navigating the inevitable changes in your world. Here's a structured approach to planning that can help leaders manage and adapt to change:

The Rank Up Step-by-Step Planning Process

Identify Potential Changes and Challenges:
- Evaluate the current market landscape and anticipate potential competitors.

- Identify internal changes that could occur as your business grows, such as the need for more staff or different expertise.

Assess Current Resources and Capabilities:
- Take stock of what resources you have—financial, human, technological—and understand how they might be affected or need to change as your business grows.

- Consider creating a resource map that details what you have and what you might need in the future.

Set Objectives for Preparedness:
- Define clear, achievable objectives for what preparedness looks like. For example, having a six-month financial buffer, cross-training staff, or establishing key partnerships.

Develop a Scalable Growth Plan:
- Plan for scaling operations that align with anticipated business growth. This could follow a specific growth pattern (e.g., expanding from one to three to seven employees) based on projected needs.

- Prepare for different scenarios that might accelerate or impede your planned growth.

Establish Contingency Measures:
- Just like setting fallback containment lines in firefighting, developing contingency plans for various business scenarios is crucial. Consider the "what ifs" that could impact your business.

- Decide in advance how you will respond if competitors enter the market or if there is a sudden economic downturn.

Allocate Roles and Responsibilities:
- Clearly define who is responsible for what within your preparedness plan. Assign team leaders and make sure they understand their responsibilities.

- Ensure that everyone knows their role in implementing the plan, similar to how a crew leader manages a team during a fire.

Schedule Regular Reviews and Updates:
- Set times to review the plan with your team, ensuring it remains relevant and effective against the backdrop of an evolving business environment.

- Use tools like whiteboards or digital apps for collaborative planning and updates.

Conduct Training and Simulation Exercises:
- Just as firefighters train for various fire scenarios, simulate business disruptions to test your team's response to unexpected changes.

- This can include role-playing a competitor entering the market or a sudden decrease in customer demand.

Implement the Plan and Monitor Progress:
- Put your preparedness plan into action. Monitor its effectiveness and make adjustments as needed.

- Keep communication lines open with your team leaders to receive regular updates and feedback on the plan's implementation.

Evaluate and Adjust Regularly:
- Regularly assess the outcome of your preparedness efforts and the relevance of your contingency plans.

- Adjust your strategies based on real-world experiences and new information to stay ahead of potential challenges.

By reframing fear as a catalyst for thorough preparation and planning, you can create a resilient business that is capable of facing and adapting to the inevitable changes and challenges of the market. This not only mitigates risks but also positions your business for sustained growth and success. Don't wait until it's too late before taking control of your risks.

If you would like to access a downloadable copy of this process as a checklist you can use in your planning, please check the list of options for resources at *FirefighterBrad.com/bookresources.*

Chapter 2:

Adapting to Change in Business

Adaptation in the face of change is a key indicator of true leadership. Leaders who can seamlessly pivot their strategies, realign their teams, and seize new opportunities are the ones who will thrive in today's volatile business world. Understanding, adapting and embracing change is not merely a strategy—it's non-negotiable if you're going to lead your people to success.

Adaptation is not about simply surviving, but about leveraging change to drive growth, innovation, and success. The future belongs to the leaders who can transform uncertainty into opportunity. This chapter looks at some specific ways businesses should adapt to endure and grow amid these inevitable shifts.

Navigating a Dynamic Environment

The digital marketing industry, which I work in, serves as a prime example of a volatile business environment. Here, search engines frequently update their algorithms to enhance user experience and penalize manipulative practices. Such changes force businesses to continually adapt their strategies to maintain visibility and relevance. Sadly, these updates can also destroy businesses that aren't watching for them.

Similarly, every industry experiences its unique pace and nature of change. From rapid technological advancements to slow shifts in consumer preferences, change is a constant companion. When you anticipate and prepare for these changes, you position yourself to seize new opportunities rather than succumb to emerging challenges.

Leadership and Adaptability

Effective leaders must also cultivate an environment where adaptability is ingrained in the organisation's culture. Your people need to be just as agile as you are if you're going to work as a team to take advantage of change as it happens. Don't look at it as an adverse event; look at it as a chance to get ahead of the competition. Here are some ways you can improve your success:

Empowering agile leadership: Leadership roles can shift depending on the task at hand. For instance, a project might see a backend coder take the lead during the development phase, while a graphic designer might step forward during the frontend execution. Recognising and empowering individuals to lead in their areas of expertise gives your people the chance to show you how capable they are. How else are you going to find your next leaders?

Building a resilient culture: Implementing regular training sessions and creating scenarios for team members to practise responding to hypothetical situations can reinforce and grow this adaptability. Fostering a culture of open communication and regular feedback also helps to identify potential areas of improvement before they become critical issues, so that the team is equipped to overcome any future problems.

Collaborative problem solving through mastermind groups: One practical approach to fostering adaptability is through mastermind groups. These small, diverse teams meet regularly to brainstorm solutions to potential problems. Each member presents their problem and, together, they develop strategies to address these challenges. This collaborative approach encourages a proactive rather than reactive mindset. The collective knowledge in the team uncovers a variety of solutions that the individuals might not have considered.

Institutional knowledge and preparedness: The concept of the Field Incident Guide (FIG) carried by firefighters can be adapted into any business setting. A comprehensive playbook that contains essential information—from operational procedures to emergency contacts—ensures that every team member can access reliable data when needed. This resource becomes particularly valuable when people are under pressure navigating unexpected changes or challenges.

Regularly updating this playbook to ensure it includes the latest strategic insights and operational tactics can help a business stay one step ahead. Additionally, training your staff to utilise this tool ensures that they are equipped to handle any situation.

Change Affects Every Business

Whether you're a solo entrepreneur or a multinational company, if you aren't alert to the changes happening in your market and don't move with them, you'll suffer the same result. Let's look at some big businesses that failed to navigate change effectively:

Borders Bookstore — Failed to adapt to the rise of e-books and the digital market; was unable to compete with platforms like Amazon's Kindle.

Yahoo — Misunderstood the power of search as Google emerged; failed to adapt to the new "index every page" technology effectively.

Holden — Struggled to adapt to global changes in the automotive industry, such as the shift towards cheaper cost of production, more fuel-efficient vehicles and electric vehicles.

Dick Smith Electronics — Failed to remain competitive in the face of changing consumer preferences for cheap, throwaway imports and the rise of online shopping.

The inevitability of change in business demands that you embrace the dynamic nature of your industries. By understanding the specific ways in which your field evolves, you can better prepare your teams for the future. Whether it's through empowering team leadership, fostering a culture of adaptability, or institutionalizing knowledge and preparedness, the goal is to turn potential disruptions into opportunities for growth and innovation.

Learning from Failure and Embracing Change

Learning from failures and embracing the resulting changes are foundational principles for growth in any field. In firefighting, a failure can have dire consequences, such as the loss of lives, properties, or both. Similarly, in business, failures can lead to significant setbacks, such as loss of clients or major contracts. However, the key to both is the same: learn, adapt, and improve.

Learning from Mistakes

As a leader, it is essential to own up to your mistakes and learn from them. This accountability is crucial not just for personal integrity but for fostering a culture of trust and continuous improvement within your team. Debriefing after projects, whether they ended in success or failure, provides valuable insights. It's not about assigning blame but about understanding what happened and how processes and decisions can be improved. Every project or task offers lessons that can drive future successes.

For instance, keeping a daily log or journal can help you track decisions and their outcomes, providing a historical context that can inform future strategies. Additionally, seeking out and learning from the failures of others can prevent similar mistakes in your own business. There are many biographies, documentaries and books that tell these stories. Engaging with a diverse network of other professionals can also help to expose you to alternative thinking, methods and strategies that may be more effective than your own.

Embracing Change through Failure

Change often comes as a direct result of failures. A failed project might reveal a flawed strategy or a gap in skills among the team, necessitating a shift in approach or enhancements in training. Flexibility and adaptability are not just beneficial traits but essential life survival skills. The structures and plans you make must be dynamic, allowing for quick adjustments as circumstances evolve.

Creating systems such as checklists and protocols helps ensure consistency and quality while leaving room for adjustments when something doesn't work as expected. These systems need to be living documents, regularly updated as new information becomes available and as your business environment changes.

Finding Opportunities in Change

Change always brings opportunities. For example, during the COVID-19 pandemic, the shift to remote work created opportunities to reduce costs on office spaces and led to happier, more productive employees due to less commuting stress. Similarly, changes in digital marketing, like updates to search engine algorithms, while initially disruptive, ultimately drive improvements in the quality of content and user experience.

It's crucial for businesses to keep abreast of industry changes and emerging trends. This can be achieved by subscribing to industry newsletters, participating in mastermind groups, attending conferences, or simply maintaining open lines of communication with clients and other stakeholders. Each of these activities offers you a heads-up to new opportunities.

Embracing change and learning from failure are intertwined concepts that drive innovation and improvement. By viewing each failure as a learning opportunity and each change as a door to new possibilities, you can cultivate a resilient and forward-thinking business culture.

As we drove onto the fireground, we were uncertain of what awaited us. The only information we had was that the area was extremely dry, creating conditions that heavily favoured the fire, not us. As per our Divisional Commander's instructions, we headed to the sector we were assigned to secure. Upon arrival, we found that the fire had reached the containment line and threatened to jump it at any moment, which would endanger nearby homes. Despite the relentless efforts of crews over the past weeks, other attempts had repeatedly failed due to adverse weather conditions.

The journey there felt like driving through a river of dust; visibility was so poor that we couldn't see the truck only ten metres ahead. The intensity of the dust was an indicator of the challenging conditions we were heading into.

Once we arrived at our designated sector, the crews dispersed and began the task of blacking out the burnt area. This involved meticulously turning over every log, breaking apart fallen trees, and drenching them until no smoke was visible. It was tedious but ensured the fire was extinguished. The more thoroughly we blacked out the area, the less likely it was for the fire to breach the containment line. A single ember was all it would take to rekindle the flames.

By then, the fire had already consumed over 7,400 hectares, and all efforts to contain it until that point had been unsuccessful.

As night fell and the winds picked up, we faced a new challenge. Tall gum trees, burning 20 to 30 metres above ground, were being fanned by the wind, causing embers to scatter across both burnt and unburnt areas. This rapidly escalated into a nightmare scenario. Crews were redeployed to monitor the unburnt areas and extinguish any new spot fires immediately.

Recognising the danger, we urgently called for chainsaw operators to fell the trees closest to the road, as they were most likely to cause further fires. The wait for their arrival was tense, but once they reached us, they efficiently and safely brought down the trees, allowing everyone to breathe a little easier. By midnight, our relief crews had arrived, and we handed over the site to them.

The following morning, we received an update from our Strike Team leader. Despite our efforts and initial success in containing the fire, it had crossed over during the night and was now threatening residential areas. The crews were back on site, protecting homes from the advancing flames.

We had thought we had achieved a victory, but it turned out we had lost that battle. It took several more days before the fire was contained. Sometimes, even when you do everything right, it's not enough to prevent failure. This incident was a harsh reminder of the unpredictability and power of nature, and how, despite our best efforts, we are not always in control.

Embrace the inevitability of change with a proactive mindset and move forward with the confidence and preparedness of an experienced leader, ready to turn challenges into triumphs. A failure is a setback, not the end. On fires, we win or we win!

Chapter 3:

How Adaptability Leads to Better Results

Driving to the shops one afternoon, I spotted a large plume of smoke rising in the distance. It was close enough that I thought we might be called out soon. Sure enough, an hour later, the fire call came through.

As we headed to the scene, darkness fell, making it difficult to see the terrain clearly. Upon arrival, we discovered the fire was burning through grass and bushland about 150 metres in from our position. The other crews were already engaged in firefighting efforts. The Incident Controller directed us down a specific track to assist, pointing out where he needed our team.

As we proceeded, we quickly encountered the challenge of the land-scape—much of the area turned out to be marshland. Multiple trucks were already bogged down in the soft soil that hampered their ability to move. One of our trucks was advised to take an alternative route but managed to get only about 50 metres before sinking up to the axles, making it impossible to proceed or extricate themselves at that moment.

Realising the truck couldn't reach the fire, the crew decided to run hoses from their halted position to the fire front. With each hose measuring 30 metres, they connected and dragged out at least 15 hoses, but their quick thinking and flexibility paid off. They managed to reach the fire front, extinguishing the flames and containing that flank. This approach required significantly more physical effort than if they had been able to drive closer, but their training and adaptability shone through, allowing us to control the fire much more quickly than anticipated.

Help eventually arrived, and all of our trucks were pulled out to solid ground. It had taken adaptability, quick thinking, and solid training to overcome unforeseen challenges. When facing demanding situations, it's crucial to utilise the resources at hand creatively and efficiently.

When leading any session, whether it's a firefighter training or a digital marketing workshop, my main goal is to empower attendees with new skills and knowledge, so that they see more potential solutions to changed situations.

This approach has been consistently successful in enhancing team dynamics and leadership effectiveness. By elevating others and focusing on collective success rather than personal gain, leaders can help their teams tackle the complexities of their work with confidence and efficiency, much like managing a well-coordinated response on the fireground.

Adapting Fireground Skills to Your Environment

My firefighting experience has honed my vigilance for hints of change—whether that's tracking trends, monitoring new software releases, or adapting to latest updates. This vigilance was cultivated on the fireground and is crucial for thriving in the digital business landscape, where rules and tools are in constant flux.

Apply Quick Decision-Making Skills

On the fireground, decisions often need to be made under life-threatening pressure. In high-stress business situations, this skill enables you to remain clear-headed and effective. Using structured decision-making tools like SMEACs (Situation, Mission, Execution, Admin & Logistics, Command & Signal) ensures that everyone on your team is aligned with a clear mission and aware of their roles and timelines, so that you complete your work and projects promptly.

Be a Calm Leader in High-Stress Situations

The most effective leaders are those who remain calm when situations are spiralling out of control. In fact, the ability to maintain composure under stress is crucial. This skill is essential for managing heated meetings or resolving conflicts within teams. In firefighting, a calm focus can often mean the difference between life and death; in business, it can mean the difference between maintaining team cohesion and being overwhelmed by chaos.

Leaders who exhibit composure when facing turmoil can inspire confidence within their team members, enabling them to make informed, rational decisions rather than reactive ones. It fosters clear-headedness and constructive solutions. Whether you're navigating a crisis or managing a high-stakes negotiation, the ability to remain calm ensures that you can steer your team toward achieving the best possible outcomes.

The Dynamics of Teamwork and Collaboration

The collaboration and communication required in effective firefighting applies directly to business. Clear communication prevents misunderstandings, and taking time to understand the client's or team's real issues before proposing solutions ensures that actions are appropriate.

One thing that firefighters do is structure our crews and fireground so that our control is not overwhelmed. You can mirror our rule of Span of Control (5-to-1) too. It will help you to optimise your communication. So how does Span of Control work and how would that help in business?

The Benefits of Span of Control (5:1)

A Span of Control, which is a fundamental concept when we're trying to contain a fire, provides a powerful framework for team management. Span of Control says that a leader or supervisor is most effective when directly overseeing no more than five to seven individuals: five people in your crew, five trucks on your sector, five sectors in a division. This structure ensures that each team member or crew receives adequate attention and guidance.

This leads to:

1. **Enhanced communication:** With fewer direct reports, leaders can spend more time with each team member or team leader. This allows for clearer and more frequent communications, ensuring that instructions are understood and feedback is timely. It reduces the risk of miscommunication, which can lead to costly errors or misaligned objectives.

2. **Improved supervision and support:** Leaders are better positioned to monitor the progress and performance of each team member or team. This close supervision helps in identifying issues early, providing targeted coaching, and offering support where needed, thereby enhancing individual performance.

3. **Increased responsiveness:** A smaller team allows for quicker decision-making and more agile responses to changing conditions. Leaders can assess and adjust strategies more swiftly without the delays that often come with larger groups.

4. **Personalised development:** Leaders can tailor development plans and career advice to the specific needs and aspirations of each team member or team. This personalised approach not

only boosts morale but also encourages professional growth, directly contributing to the team's overall capabilities.

5. **Stronger relationships:** Smaller teams foster closer relationships and better trust between leaders and their reports. This can lead to deeper engagement and commitment, as team members feel more valued and understood.

Implementing this structure will help you to create a more engaged, productive, and cohesive group, facilitating success in any high-stakes environment.

Simple Steps to Implement Span of Control

- **Team structuring:** When setting up teams, especially in larger organisations, it's helpful to design the hierarchy to work to this ratio. This might mean creating more layers within departments, which will lead to more effective management and oversight.

- **Leadership training:** Your leaders should be trained not only to manage their direct reports effectively but also to understand the benefits of span of control. Training needs to include skills in delegation, communication, conflict resolution, and motivation to empower them to manage their small teams effectively.

- **Feedback mechanisms:** Implement regular feedback loops within these small teams. This could be through one-on-ones, team meetings, or performance reviews. The aim is to ensure that leaders are continuously aligned with their team members and can provide the necessary support to meet their objectives.

- **Technology support:** Use technology to streamline communication and management processes. Tools like project management software, instant messaging platforms, and performance tracking systems can help leaders stay on top of their responsibilities without becoming overwhelmed.

By mirroring the firefighter's approach using span of control (5:1), you can create an environment where your leaders are more effective, team members are better supported, and the organisation as a whole becomes more adaptable and successful. This strategic structuring of teams optimises operational efficiency and also enhances overall workplace satisfaction and productivity.

*If you need to implement the 5:1 span of control with your organisation or team leaders, here's a straightforward exercise you can do with a group of 5 or more people. It works just as well with one, but a brilliant group dynamic kicks in when you get to do this as a team. If you need help with developing this with your team, I can also direct you to **FirefighterBrad.com/training**, where you will find more information about how I can work with you to make this happen.*

Exercise: Implementing Span of Control (5:1) in Your Team

This section provides a step-by-step guide on conducting a 30-minute exercise to begin integrating this concept into your business or firefighting unit. Effective span of control on incidents may vary from three to seven, but a ratio of one leader to five reporting elements is recommended.

Preparation

Materials Needed:

Whiteboard or flip chart
Markers
Sticky notes

Set-up:

- Arrange the meeting space to accommodate small groups of 5–7 leaders each.

- Prepare the whiteboard or flip chart at the front for visibility.

Execution

Step 1: Introduction (5 minutes)

- Start the session by explaining the concept of Span of Control (5:1), emphasizing its origin in firefighting where it ensures effective management and safety.

- Use the diagram below to demonstrate how it works.

- Highlight the benefits of this model in a business context, focusing on improved direct supervision, distributed leadership and more personalised team management.

Step 2: Quick Assessment (5 minutes)

- Ask each leader to quickly assess & draw out their current team structure. Have them note the number of direct reports they manage and identify one primary challenge this structure creates.

- This step raises awareness of their current management load and surfaces potential issues related to having too many direct reports.

Step 3: Brainstorming (10 minutes)
- Instruct your leaders to brainstorm practical ways to restructure their teams to achieve the 5:1 ratio. (Note: maximum span of control is commonly 7). Use sticky notes for jotting down ideas or draw it out on paper.

- Leaders should think about which roles are essential and how they can be grouped effectively to enhance management and oversight.

Step 4: Drafting a Quick Action Plan (5 minutes)
- From the brainstorming, ask each leader to choose one actionable step they can implement to start adjusting their span of control.

- Have them write this step on a sticky note and share it with the group, explaining why they chose this step and how they anticipate it will help.

- This may not always be possible but encourage them to do their best to achieve the goal.

Step 5: Group Feedback (3 minutes)
- Conduct a rapid-fire feedback session, where each leader provides a quick critique or enhancement suggestion for another leader's plan.

- This peer review fosters collaborative thinking and can refine the approaches being considered.

Step 6: Commitment and Conclusion (2 minutes)
- Encourage each leader to commit to a date by which they will enact their chosen plan. This commitment should be voiced to the group to encourage accountability.

- Conclude the session by reinforcing the value of adaptability and structured leadership, and how these are crucial for both firefighting and business success.

Follow-Up

- Recommend that leaders schedule a follow-up meeting with their teams to discuss the implementation of these changes.

- Suggest keeping a diary or log to record the impacts of these changes, which can be reviewed in future team meetings or leadership training sessions.

This exercise is designed to be a quick initiation into rethinking and reshaping team management structures. By starting with a single, manageable change, leaders can gradually work towards fully implementing span of control, significantly enhancing their leadership effectiveness and team success.

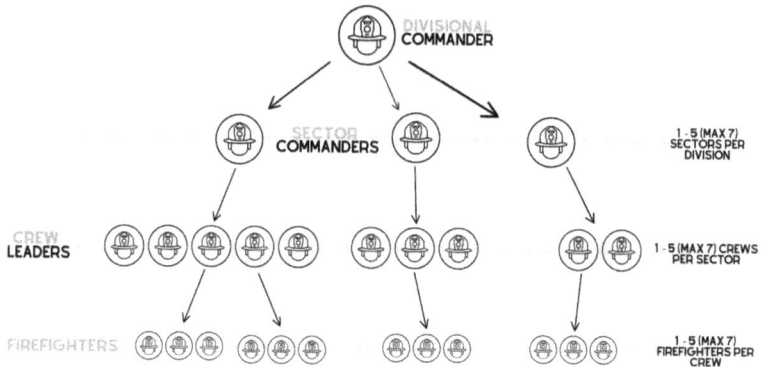

DIVISIONAL COMMANDER

SECTOR COMMANDERS

1 - 5 (MAX 7) SECTORS PER DIVISION

CREW LEADERS

1 - 5 (MAX 7) CREWS PER SECTOR

FIREFIGHTERS

1 - 5 (MAX 7) FIREFIGHTERS PER CREW

Adaptable Teams Are More Effective

By integrating some common firefighting principles into your leadership—leveraging teamwork, managing stress and fear through experience, and learning rigorously from both successes and failures—you can build resilient organisations capable of thriving in today's dynamic environments.

The Role of Teamwork

A proactive mindset is crucial. Being constantly aware and attuned to the subtle shifts within your environment allows you to preempt crises. This heightened awareness is a quality honed over time—more experience brings greater perceptiveness. For business leaders, staying informed through a range of channels such as news, podcasts, and networking isn't about knowledge; it's about gaining an edge. Engaging in meaningful conversations with other leaders can shed light on industry trends, potential challenges, and innovative solutions. Effective teamwork is about using every piece of this information to coordinate and enhance collective efforts, ensuring that both fireground operations and business projects are handled efficiently.

Three things you can do to raise the standard of teamwork in your organisation:

- Proactive awareness: Cultivate a habit of constant vigilance. Notice the small changes and subtle cues in your environment to anticipate and mitigate potential problems before they escalate. As a firefighter, I'm looking for changes in wind, humidity, available crews and many other conditions as they can develop quickly into major issues.

- Continuous learning: Stay updated with the latest industry trends, news, and technologies. Utilize diverse information sources like podcasts, articles, and professional networks to stay ahead of the curve. There are so many sources of quality information available today but you just need to cherry pick the most useful sources.

- Information sharing: Encourage open communication within your team. Share insights and knowledge from external interactions to enhance collective understanding and response strategies. Learn to keep sharing information as you come across it. Everyone observes different changes, and they're all important to your success as a team.

Managing Fear and High-Stress Decisions

Fear is a huge contributor to high-stress situations, whether responding to a bushfire or navigating critical business decisions. The key to managing fear is getting more experience. The more challenging situations you face, the more adept you become at handling them. In firefighting, repeated exposure to high-stress situations like fire calls reduces fear, allowing you to think more clearly and to take more decisive action. The strategies we use in firefighting like rigorous training and simulations can also be applied in business to prepare you to act confidently under pressure and make informed decisions swiftly.

Three things you can do to help manage fear when your team is highly stressed:

- **Develop confidence through exposure:** Regularly expose yourself and your team to stressful scenarios in controlled settings to decrease anxiety and improve performance under pressure.

- **Participate in strategic training:** Implement training methods that simulate high-stress situations similar to those encountered in firefighting, such as role-playing or crisis management exercises. Introduce unexpected challenges to stretch people beyond their current capabilities.

- **Encourage quick decision-making:** Foster an environment where decisions need to be made swiftly yet thoughtfully, mirroring the demands of a fireground operation.

Learning from Failures

Whether a project succeeds or stumbles, taking the time to review what happened is invaluable. Business leaders can learn from firefighters by always conducting thorough debriefs to analyse the major decisions made and the outcomes. This practice should use four main questions:

1. What was planned?
2. What really happened?
3. Why did it happen?
4. What can we do better next time?

It's not merely about scrutinising failures but about understanding and replicating successes. These lessons are then integrated into future strategies, continually refining processes and enhancing team performance.

Failure is part of any successful leader's education. It would be preferrable to never fail, but that's just not realistic. Prussian general Field Marshall Helmuth von Moltke is famously quoted as saying, *"No plan survives first contact with the enemy. It might be painful at the time, but these are learning opportunities."*

The second website I ever built turned out to be a huge success. It started as a small site for teachers, featuring about 20 certificate templates they could download, fill in, and print for their students. Titles included "Student of the Week," "Best Book Report," "100% Homework Completed", and so on. What began as a modest project quickly grew, with over a thousand teachers a day downloading certificates for their classes.

While teaching at the time, I kept adding any new certificates I made for my class to the site. The traffic continued to grow, and I eventually transformed it into a lifetime membership for $29, turning it into a profitable income stream. By then, the site was attracting about 10 million visitors a month. The experience of building this site and optimising its SEO would later inspire me to start my own business, offering search engine ranking services for local and international companies.

As my new business grew, I left the website to run on autopilot. That's something that I would never allow a fire to do and I should have known better. The site was self-sustaining, requiring only regular content updates based on popular search terms among teachers. It consistently ranked #1 globally, and the income continued to flow.

Then, one day, everything changed.

Logging in to check my stats, I saw that sales had stopped. Something was drastically wrong. Since there were no recent Google algorithm changes, I suspected a problem with the site code. However, upon checking, everything was working fine. Puzzled, I did a Google search to check my rankings. To my horror, I was no longer in the Top 10. Another search revealed that my site wasn't appearing in the search results at all. I felt sick. I hadn't done anything differently—there was no "black hat" SEO involved. *Everything had been consistent, yet my site had been "Google slapped".*

I did everything I could to restore the site's rankings. Unfortunately, Google doesn't disclose reasons for such penalties. Despite my efforts, the site never regained its position. This "slap" cost me millions in lost revenue over the following years.

By this time this happened, I had been fighting fires for several fire seasons and had been trained to prepare for our best plans to fail. Because of that I had anticipated that it was possible for a website to fail, even if I did everything right, and I had diversified by building other sites and income streams. While it broke my heart to see that business stream die, being prepared meant it didn't put me out of business.

After You Win or You Lose

Debriefing plays a pivotal role in accepting change and enhances future preparedness and performance. In firefighting, the practice of conducting thorough debriefs after every call allows teams to analyse their actions, learn from mistakes, and reinforce successful strategies. This process ensures that each experience, whether a routine operation or a high-stakes emergency, contributes to the team's evolving expertise.

Similarly, you should be debriefing after projects or major decisions as it provides a structured opportunity to review outcomes, discuss what could have been done differently, and affirm practices that led to success. This fosters a culture of continuous improvement and accountability; it also helps refine project management strategies, ensuring teams are better equipped to handle future challenges.

I call this the DADA Process: Debrief — Analyse — Document — Adapt. I invite you to use it to build a culture of positive debriefing in your organisation.

- **Debrief:** Make it standard practice to conduct debriefing sessions after every major project or significant decision, regardless of the outcome.

- **Analyse:** In debriefs, focus on analysing what was planned, what actually happened, why it happened, and identify opportunities for improvement.

- **Document:** Keep detailed records of all debriefings to track patterns and progress over time. These records are of the facts and should not contain names, as we aren't looking to assign blame.

- **Adapt:** Use these insights to refine strategies and improve operations on a continuous basis.

Dealing with Change

"Face the winds of change like a firefighter faces a wildfire: with readiness, resolve, and the relentless pursuit of success!"

Chapter 4:

Humour as a Coping Mechanism

As I touched on briefly in the last chapter, coping with fear, changes, and high stress can be a significant issue for you as a leader, and I'd like to share some of the ways I have learned from firefighting that I've also adapted successfully into my businesses when dealing with rapid change.

Laughter Helps

In the thick of high-stress situations, finding humour can be a lifeline, a way to cope when the heat is on—both literally and metaphorically. I've always been the kind of person who finds a laugh in the midst of chaos. It's my way to manage stress, and over the years, I've found it can lighten the load for others too.

A few years back, during a gruelling deployment in the country, my crew and I were tasked with containing a stubborn bushfire. We had been at it all day in the thick of the flames and the smoke, and, as dusk fell, exhaustion was setting in. We were supposed to be relieved by a new crew at 17:00, but hours ticked by with no sign of them.

Frustration was mounting. Tired, hungry, and irritated, we sat in our air-conditioned trucks which were surrounded by smoke, breathing in the fresh air and waiting for a reprieve.

Amidst the growing tension, our phones pinged with a notification from our deployment's Facebook Messenger group—a tool we used for quick updates and info sharing when out of radio reach. Expecting news of our relief, I checked the message, hoping for some end to our long wait. Instead, what popped up was a photo of a rock. Yes, a rock. Under any other circumstances, it might have seemed trivial, even irritatingly so, but not this time.

Laughter erupted in our truck, spreading quickly as the others checked their phones. This wasn't just any rock; it was humorously shaped like a human backside. The sender had dubbed it "Bum Rock", capturing the image earlier that day but only now sharing the levity with us all. The comments rolled in, lightening everyone's spirits. "Spotted Bum Rock but didn't have time to stop, so here's a quick snap."

The jokes and banter about Bum Rock breathed new life into our weary group. Plans were even hatched to visit the rock the next day for a group photo, turning our shared amusement into a mini-mission. Though my crew never made it back to Bum Rock, the image and the laughs it brought remained a high point of that deployment. Over the next few days, every similar rock became a welcome sight, a reason to chuckle amidst the smoke and fatigue.

This experience reinforced a valuable lesson: never underestimate the power of humour, especially when the going gets tough. A simple laugh can transform the mood, turning gruelling tasks into bearable ones. It reminds us that joy can be found in the smallest moments, and sometimes, a good laugh is the best kind of relief. As we face life's fires, it's the moments of fun like Bum Rock that keep our spirits high and our hearts light.

Embracing humour is not just a relief strategy; I've found

it essential for maintaining mental health amidst rapid change. Understand that humour manifests differently for everyone—what makes one person chuckle might not elicit even a smile from another. It's crucial to discover what tickles your funny bone, whether it's through memes, photos, movies, jokes, podcasts, or simply swapping stories with your team. These moments of laughter can allow everyone a chance to breathe and find joy in the absurdities of life.

The ability to laugh at yourself and take a joke from your team is invaluable. Working with someone who lacks a sense of humour, who takes every comment to heart, creates a tense and uncomfortable environment. Leaders should lead by example; admitting to and laughing off your own mistakes can endear you to your team and set a tone of humility and openness. For instance, it's a running joke that no fire call is complete without me tripping over something and ending up lying on the ground. Acknowledging this trait has become part of our team's camaraderie—it's expected, it's laughed off, and then we move on.

In your workplace, humour must be handled sensitively and appropriately. Simple things like sharing a funny meme or using emojis in communications can brighten someone's day, but it's crucial to understand your team's dynamics and respect boundaries. Humour in the workplace has evolved significantly—what was once acceptable banter in a predominantly male team might not be appropriate in today's diverse work environments. The goal is to foster inclusivity, not alienation. If a joke or comment doesn't sit well with everyone, then it's no joke at all.

Creating a workplace where laughter and levity are part of the culture is a leadership responsibility. Organise social events that are optional but fun, celebrate team successes, acknowledge personal milestones like birthdays, and make an effort to personally connect with your team members. These activities not only boost morale but also reinforce a sense of belonging. For many, the workplace is their primary social sphere, and feeling connected and valued can transform their professional and personal lives. Leaders who can cultivate a sense of community and show genuine care for their team's well-being will inspire loyalty and dedication that transcends the ordinary bonds of a workplace.

Here are 5 easy ways to introduce more humour into your team or workplace:

Building humour into your workplace culture can significantly enhance team cohesion and overall job satisfaction, but you must consider every member of your team. Here are five tips for integrating humour in a respectful and inclusive manner:

1. **Lead by example:** Demonstrate your own sense of humour by sharing light-hearted stories or appropriate jokes about your own experiences. Show that it's okay to laugh at your own harmless mistakes. This sets a tone of humility and approachability within the team.

2. **Create a "fun committee":** Establish a committee dedicated to organizing fun, informal activities that encourage laughter and relaxation. This could range from themed office days to casual after-work gatherings. A variety of events ensures that different senses of humour and interests are accommodated, allowing everyone to participate, if they choose, in something that resonates with them.

3. **Encourage sharing of light content:** Invite team members to share amusing, work-appropriate content, whether it's comics, memes, or funny videos that can be enjoyed over lunch or during breaks. This not only injects humour into the workplace but also allows team members to share a bit of their personality.

4. **Integrate humour into communications:** Use light-hearted language in internal communications where appropriate. This could be as simple as a emoticon in an email or a humorous

observation in a newsletter. Such practices can help lighten the mood and make routine communications more engaging.

5. **Celebrate the silly:** Recognize and celebrate "silly" holidays that relate to your industry or team interests. For example, if you're in the tech industry, you might celebrate "Embrace Your Geekness Day". These small celebrations can provide a fun break from the norm and a chance for everyone to engage in some light-hearted fun.

By thoughtfully integrating humour into your leadership style and workplace culture, you can help create an environment where team members feel more connected and less stressed, improving both morale and productivity.

Chapter 5:

Developing a Change Mindset through Training

In firefighting, rigorous and consistent training serves as the backbone of our ability to perform under pressure and manage the unpredictable nature of fire emergencies. When our brigade meets for weekly training, it is to engage in structured training sessions that are meticulously planned weeks or months in advance. This regularity not only ensures that each firefighter develops a comprehensive set of skills but also fosters a culture of continuous improvement and readiness. From practical exercises at the station to complex scenario-based simulations, our training programs are designed to instil competence and boost confidence, enabling each member to manage live fire situations safely and skilfully.

Training is not just about learning the ropes; it's about preparing to handle whatever challenges come your way. It transforms a group of individuals into a cohesive crew ready to tackle fires and other incidents.

Here's how we do it, and how these methods can be translated into powerful practices in the business world.

Firefighter training:

Building competence and confidence — How *we* do it!

- **Regular, scheduled training:** In our brigade, training is every Tuesday night. This consistency allows us to prepare in advance, cycling through different trainers and topics to build a well-rounded skill set.

- **Diverse training methods:** We employ a mix of online theory, classroom learning and practical, scenario-based practice. These scenarios range from simple exercises like extinguishing a "fire" represented by a traffic cone, to complex simulations involving multiple teams and dynamic challenges such as equipment failures or a sudden burnover drills—unexpected to the crews.

- **Debriefing:** After each training session, we gather to discuss what went well and what didn't. This enhances immediate learning and also cultivates an environment where feedback is used constructively to improve ourselves both as learners and trainers.

Translating Firefighting Training to Business Leadership — How you can too!

- **Adapt training to fit your team:** Like new firefighters, new employees bring diverse backgrounds and skills. Tailored training programs ensure they understand not just their roles but also the culture and processes of your company.

- **Create realistic business scenarios:** Just as we simulate fire scenarios, businesses can benefit from scenario-based training. These can include new trends, product launches, or even internal crises, preparing your team to think on their feet.

- **Foster a learning environment:** Encourage your employees to lead training sessions in their areas of expertise. This not only boosts their confidence but also enhances team knowledge and cohesion.

In the fast-paced world of business, fostering a mindset that embraces change is crucial for staying competitive and innovative. As leaders, it is imperative we cultivate an environment where continuous learning and adaptability are at the core. This involves not only staying abreast of trends and advancements but also actively engaging every team member in the learning and training delivery process. By implementing strategies that encourage feedback, utilise diverse skill sets, and promote an ongoing dialogue about improvements, businesses can adjust to external demands and internal challenges. These are some effective strategies to embed a change mindset deeply within your business framework, ensuring that your organisation (and its leadership team) not only survives but thrives.

Strategies for Fostering a Change Mindset in Business

- **Continuous learning**: Stay informed about industry trends and encourage your team to do the same. This could be through workshops, seminars, or curated content relevant to your industry.

- **Engage in feedback loops**: Regular feedback sessions help you tap into the diverse experiences and insights of your team, allowing for continuous improvement and adaptation.

- **Recognise and utilise diverse skill sets**: Every member of your team has unique skills and knowledge. By leveraging these diverse abilities, you can enhance your team's overall performance and adaptability.

Implementing Effective Training in Your Business

By fostering a robust training environment, you equip your team not just to meet expectations but to exceed them, no matter what challenges they face. As their leader, it's your responsibility to ensure that your team is not only prepared for today but also equipped for the uncertainties of tomorrow.

So, how do you go about ensuring that you have effective training programs in your organisation that everyone engages in and even gets excited about?

Here are three easy ways to do this:

1. **Schedule regular sessions:** Incorporate short, frequent training sessions into your regular business schedule. These should be interactive and engaging to maintain attention and enhance learning. Regularity breeds expectation.

2. **Encourage participation:** Have *every* team member take a turn leading sessions on topics they are passionate about. This not only improves their skills but also helps others learn new aspects of the business.

3. **Monitor and adapt:** Regularly assess the impact of your training. What skills have improved? What areas still need attention? Adapt your training programs based on this feedback to meet the continually evolving needs of your business.

In firefighting, where the demands are intensely physical and the risks exceptionally high, training transcends typical job preparation—it is about survival, competence, and the confidence to face intense situations. Regular training sessions, as practised in my brigade, underscore the importance of not only maintaining skills but continuously advancing them. By adopting a structured approach to training, where sessions are planned out in advance and include both theory and practice, you can ensure that your team members are not just reacting to challenges but are well prepared to anticipate and tackle them.

The pace of change in business can be relentless, and companies that equip their employees to handle and even anticipate it can maintain a competitive edge. Training should go beyond onboarding new hires; it should be an ongoing process that encourages lifelong learning and continuous improvement for all members of your team, especially yourself! By engaging team members in training that keeps them abreast of industry trends, your workforce will be not only adept at managing current roles but also prepared to take on anything the world throws at them. This initiative-taking approach enriches the organisation's culture, making it a vibrant, dynamic, and forward-thinking environment where learning is seen as integral to everyday operations.

Far too often, companies think of training as being what you do when someone joins the company or something you complete externally as part of your required professional development requirements only. That's not doing your business or your key personnel any favours. Growth will only come from having well-trained people from bottom to top.

Upon arriving at the station for training, we discovered that the water pump on one of our fire trucks had been upgraded. The original petrol pump had been replaced with a diesel one, which was deemed safer and more powerful. Having grown accustomed to the old pump, we started the night with drills focused on operating the new system— starting it, getting water out to the hose reels, and then stopping it. These basic yet essential skills are critical for any firefighter; obviously, knowing how to start the pump is key to our ability to extinguish fires.

After we had repeated the process on multiple trucks, one of the other officers posed a question: did anyone know what to do if the pump ran dry; i.e., ran out of fuel? Our previous experience had been with petrol pumps that could simply be refilled to restart. That's when I learnt that diesel pumps operated differently—they needed to be bled. Initially, I assumed this would be a complex task, but it turned out to be quite straightforward: just undo a locking screw, loosen a bolt until fuel begins to seep out, and then secure everything back in place. The simplicity of the task surprised me; all I needed to remember were the two different spanner sizes, which, fortunately, coincided with my birthdate and wedding anniversary.

About a month later, during a fire, I encountered a crew struggling with their truck's pump. They explained that even after being refilled, the pump wouldn't restart. With the fire dangerously approaching, they were close to leaving to get it fixed. Identifying the pump as the same diesel model we had at our station, I quickly retrieved the correct spanners from my truck. Within 30 seconds, the pump was operational again.

This experience was a potent reminder of how invaluable training can be. At that critical moment, I was able to keep an essential crew on the fire line, where we desperately needed their support. It underscored the importance of thorough training—from recruits to officers—ensuring that everyone knows how to effectively address such problems.

Motivation and Resilience Come from the Training Ground Too

In high-pressure environments, resilience is often thought of as a trait that you either have or you don't. However, true resilience is cultivated over time through consistent exposure to challenging situations. It is a blend of inherent character and learned behaviour, and it's shaped significantly during times of crisis.

During the devastating Black Summer fires in Australia during 2019/2020, firefighters were pushed to their limits of endurance. My brigade was on the front lines for almost 122 days straight, a gruelling test of both mental and physical stamina. This period wasn't about combatting flames; it was a profound lesson in maintaining motivation under relentless stress. The sheer length of the crisis meant that traditional motivators like adrenaline and positive thinking were insufficient. Instead, what sustained us was a deeply held collective mission: to protect our community from the destruction that a fire brings. This shared purpose provided the drive needed to persevere through exhaustion and danger.

This principle holds equally true in business. The most effective way to foster resilience within a team is to unite them under a mission that transcends the pursuit of profits. It must be a goal that resonates on a deeper level, encouraging individuals to push through challenges not just for personal gain, but for a common good. Leadership in such scenarios goes beyond directing people's actions; it involves you building trust and demonstrating commitment to the team's welfare and the mission's success.

In times of crisis, your instinct might be to drive your team relentlessly. However, resilience is also about knowing when to pull back and how to pace the team to prevent burnout. Celebrating small victories and acknowledging your team's hard work are crucial for sustaining morale and motivation. It's important to remember that resilience isn't just about endurance; it's about adapting strategically to prolonged stressors while maintaining team cohesion and individual well-being.

Understanding the personal needs of your team members plays a critical role in their performance and their success. Just as we manage our firefighting duties around our jobs and families, you must recognise the personal demands on your employees. True leadership involves helping team members find balance, not just pushing them to their limits. It's about knowing when to say no and when to encourage a break, ensuring that resilience is built sustainably across all aspects of people's lives.

When you regularly spend time together in training environments, you get to know who has what strengths and weaknesses, and also where your leaders need development. Regular training also helps everyone to know who to turn to when things go wrong, who to count on, and how far to push some people. Not everyone is built to deal with elevated levels of stress, so it's important that you monitor your team members. A resilience mindset developed through constant teamwork is your best line of defence against challenging situations in any environment.

Your training strategy is a plan that helps you to further develop and lean into your mission as an organisation. You can identify and highlight skills and find the leaders who will take your mission and drive it further.

Cultivating a change mindset through rigorous training, teamwork, and exposure to unpredictable situations prepares you to manage and adapt to crises effectively. This approach not only enhances individual and team resilience but also ensures that your organisation is robust enough to withstand and thrive amidst challenges.

Chapter 6:

Loyalty, Trust, and Communication

In any dynamic and unpredictable situation, the key elements of loyalty, trust, and effective communication are vital in dealing with change. When crises arise and situations deteriorate rapidly, the ability to rely on the team around you becomes crucial. Cultivating loyalty is a two-way street: if you show that you genuinely care for and support your team, they will reciprocate with commitment and a readiness to collaborate under any circumstances. This principle held true during the gruelling 122 days of the Black Summer fires, where the bonds of loyalty and mutual trust among my brigade's firefighters were tested to their limits.

Loyalty in the fire service extends directly to the individuals themselves. It is built through shared experiences and a common mission, creating a deep-seated allegiance that does not waver, even when members crew together after months apart. Similarly, in business, loyalty is not just about aligning with the company's goals but also about fostering a direct, trusting relationship with each team member. As a leader, you must encourage an open environment where team members feel safe to voice concerns, offer ideas, and know that their contributions are valued. This openness strengthens trust and empowers team members, reinforcing their commitment to the organisation's objectives.

Effective communication is another cornerstone of successful leadership, particularly evident in firefighting where conditions can change in an instant. During a deployment in a rural area unfamiliar to my team and me, the challenge of fighting a bushfire was made more difficult by the unexpected occurrence of spot fires caused by wind-carried embers landing far from the main fire line starting fires hundreds of metres behind us. In our local area, we didn't normally encounter this. This experience underscored the importance of maintaining constant vigilance and adapting our strategies to the local conditions.

In business, just as on the fireground, understanding the nuances of your environment and the specific challenges your team faces is crucial. You must facilitate clear, ongoing communication and be adept at interpreting the signals of both the market and your team members. Regular training and shared experiences can significantly enhance situational awareness, enhancing your team's ability to navigate the complexities of some business projects.

Loyalty, trust, and effective communication are the very fabric that holds teams together, whether battling a ferocious bushfire or steering a company through turbulent times. They ensure that every team member is aligned, feels supported, and is fully engaged in the mission at hand. By embodying these qualities, leaders can inspire their teams to achieve more than they thought possible.

Cultivating a Culture of Communication

Communication is the cornerstone of a resilient and loyal team, whether on the fireground or in the corporate office. As a leader, it's your responsibility to ensure clear communication flows freely up, down and sideways to reach all members of your team. Their functionality can be improved or hindered by how well your messages move through your organisation.

Communication within a fire brigade must be clear and precise, especially when tackling unfamiliar challenges in new environments. While fighting a bushfire in a region characterised by dry conditions and unpredictable winds, our team had to quickly adapt to the unexpected challenge of spot fires, which were unfamiliar to us based on our usual experiences. This required a heightened level of teamwork and communication. We had to observe more diligently and coordinate more closely than ever, ensuring that no new threats were overlooked. The minute that anyone on the team observed a smoke plume behind us, all firefighters were alerted by radio so that we could organise a response.

In business settings, you should strive to understand the unique dynamics of your team and the environments they operate in. This involves not only directing tasks but also actively listening, encouraging feedback, and ensuring that all team members have the information necessary to perform their roles. Acknowledging the diverse backgrounds and skills within a team can lead to more innovative solutions and stronger relationships, enhancing the team's overall performance.

My business has built many websites over the years. During that time, I have learnt a lot about what to do and what not to do when working with clients on their sites. One thing that other business owners warned me about was "scope creep". Scope creep happens when you agree to do a project, but during the process, the client changes their requirements. In the case of websites, they might want to alter the template, integrate their social media, or change the colours.

Whatever it is, it frequently means redoing huge chunks of the project from scratch. What seems like a simple task becomes a huge one. The real issue is that they want "just this little change", and because you've agreed on a price for the project, you end up doing it for free, even though it costs you time and money.

After dealing with this a couple of times, I decided I couldn't afford to keep losing so much money. It was my fault, not the client's. I realised that communications had broken down between us. If the same thing had happened on a fire, I would have been doing everything I could to reestablish that link so I could talk to our crews but being in business, I had just accepted it as normal.

I had not communicated clearly enough the specific contents of the project—and exactly what the price included. I had not clearly communicated that any extras would require more time and money. Finally, I had not ensured that they agreed to the specifics of the design brief before signing the contract, so that we all knew what the result would look like.

To overcome this, I developed a specific template to add to my contract, listing all the components of the website and their details. I would go through all of these individually with the client and tick them off. Finally, I added a statement that made it crystal clear that any work outside this scope, as agreed by them, would be charged at an hourly rate of a minimum of $200. This certainly caught their attention.

It worked. From then on, my clients and I had a clear understanding of their project, and I didn't have any more problems with scope creep. By accepting that this was a problem I caused through poor communication, I was able to overcome it, and everyone was happy with the work we delivered.

By fostering a culture where communication is valued and trust is built through consistent actions, you can create teams that are more able to achieve the organisation's overarching goals and keep your clients happy. Whether you're responding to a fire or not, the ability to communicate effectively, understand each other's strengths and weaknesses, and work towards a shared mission is invaluable. The power of communication is more than just being able to get a message from one person to another. It becomes the glue that keeps your team together.

How to Ensure a Culture of Communication

Cultivating an ethos of clear communication within any team—whether in firefighting, business, or any other field—requires deliberate and consistent effort.

Here's my five-step guide to help leaders establish and nurture this crucial aspect of team dynamics:

Step 1: Establish Clear Communication Channels

- **Define the main channels** through which official communication will occur, such as meetings, emails, memos, and instant messaging platforms.

- **Ensure accessibility,** so that every team member can easily reach out when necessary.

- **Set some basic rules** to keep general chatter in its rightful place and other aspects like restricting out-of-hours messaging.

- **Establish lines** of communication and ensure that these channels are always open, fostering an environment where team members feel comfortable sharing their thoughts and feedback.

Step 2: Promote Transparency

- **Be open about goals, challenges, and decisions.** Keeping team members in the loop on key business activities and decisions builds trust and helps align efforts.

- **Encourage managers and team leaders** to share valuable information regularly, eliminating any ambiguity about business processes or expectations.

- **Handle sensitive information with care** but strive to be as open as possible to avoid rumours and misinformation.

Step 3: Foster a Culture of Feedback

- **Implement regular feedback cycles** where employees can

share their thoughts on their work environment, management, and overall job satisfaction.

- **Encourage constructive feedback** not only from top to bottom but also from bottom to top, where people feel safe to express concerns and make suggestions.

- **Act on the feedback received,** showing that the organization values and uses employee input to make improvements.

Step 4: Develop Active Listening Skills

- **Train leaders and managers** in active listening techniques, ensuring they fully understand and consider team input before responding.

- **Encourage empathy** by reminding all team members to consider the feelings and viewpoints of others, which can enhance interpersonal relationships and team cohesion.

- **Practice active listening in every interaction,** demonstrating commitment to understanding each other fully and building a supportive team environment.

Step 5: Celebrate and Reinforce Effective Communication

- **Recognize and reward examples** of effective communication within the team. This could be through formal awards or informal acknowledgments in meetings.

- **Share success stories** where effective communication led to successful outcomes, reinforcing the value of these efforts.

- **Regularly review and refresh communication strategies** to ensure they remain effective and adjust to new challenges or changes within the organization.

By following these steps, you can cultivate a strong ethos of communication that enhances operational efficiency and contributes to a more engaged and connected team. This foundation of trust and openness is essential for any organisation to thrive in today's often unpredictable environments.

Even with the best systems and communication technology in place, the effectiveness of a team can be compromised if these are not applied properly.

This lesson came to life during a large fire where our Strike Team leader decided to split us into two sector teams, each assigned a different radio channel for communication. The plan was for each team to be deployed to separate areas for backburning, but as events unfolded, we all ended up working together in the same sector. This change led to confusion, as trucks were intermingled along the fire line trying to communicate on their original assigned channels.

The breakdown in communication became critical when the radio signal started to break down. Positioned at the tail end of the group, my crew was cut off from those in front because the radio kept dropping in and out. This issue persisted for several hours. Although I could still see the truck ahead, the increasing distance and intensity of the fire made direct communication impossible. We reached out to our Sector Commander, voicing our concerns and requesting a unified channel. Unfortunately, he informed us that his request for this change had been denied by the Strike Team leader.

As the evening approached, visibility worsened, and we completely lost sight of and communication with the trucks in front. It was then that another truck unexpectedly approached from behind, and the Crew Leader, surprised to find us there, informed us that our teams had left the fireground over half an hour earlier. We were inadvertently left behind due to the communication failures, and the oversight was not realised by anyone in our group.

This incident highlighted a serious safety breach. Upon reconnecting with our Strike Team, we discovered widespread discontent and frustration with our Strike Team leader's decisions, which had exacerbated the day's challenges and risks. His persistent refusal to consolidate communication channels the following day forced us to adapt independently, setting up a secondary radio channel without his approval to ensure we could maintain contact.

From this experience, I learned the critical importance of effective communication for safety and the value of listening to your team leaders. They are often the first to know when systems fail, and if their advice is ignored, team members may resort to solving problems on their own, potentially compromising both safety and structure.

When you're leading a team, especially in high-pressure environments, ensuring open lines of communication and taking the advice of experienced team members can prevent not only operational failures but also protect everyone involved. Communication is everyone's responsibility but we must set the example for others to follow.

Chapter 7:

The Power in Adaptable Teams

Crewing Dynamics in Firefighting

When you are a volunteer firefighter, the unpredictability of crew composition is a given. It changes every time we turn out, so we train our people to accept it. When the pager sounds, we rush to the station, and the person who arrives first often determines the initial crew make-up. Our app shows who is responding, but distance from the station means you never know who will be on hand when it's time to roll out. Typically, the first three people to arrive head out in the first truck, and so on, although this can vary depending on the need for specific roles or team configurations. This system ensures that every call could mean a new team dynamic, adding a layer of complexity and excitement to every response.

The unpredictable nature of our crewing teaches us profound lessons in adaptability. We might not see some team members for months due to varying schedules, yet the bonds of loyalty and trust we forge during fires hold strong. This adaptability is crucial not only in firefighting but also in business environments. In both settings, we must ensure we can count on our teams, and the teams must trust each other to make decisions that will protect and benefit everyone. This trust is built over time and through shared experiences, becoming particularly evident during crises.

On the fireground, adaptability is continuously tested. For instance, it's not uncommon to switch crews multiple times in a single day depending on the fire's demands and tactical needs. Each change requires quick adjustment and immediate teamwork, even with those you've never worked alongside previously. Being thrust into a new group as an Officer or Crew Leader adds another layer of challenge—you must quickly establish trust and demonstrate competence.

Deployment away from your usual brigade area highlights the need for adaptability. Firefighters are often grouped with peers from various brigades for extended missions, requiring rapid relationship building and team cohesion. This scenario is akin to project teams who might be assembled from different departments or locations, necessitating swift acclimatisation to the new dynamics and personalities.

Leaders must be ready to manage unexpected changes with confidence and decisiveness. By fostering a culture that values quick adaptation and mutual support, you can create resilient teams capable of facing any challenge, whether it's a raging wildfire or shifting client demands. This adaptability is not just about survival; it's about thriving in the face of adversity and building bonds that enhance collective strength and loyalty.

Applying the Concept of Crewing to Business Teams

The concept of crewing in firefighting, where adaptability and swift team formation are critical, offers a range of valuable lessons in leadership and team management. In a business, applying the principle of random crewing can enhance project execution, improve team dynamics, and increase overall organisational resilience as people become used to working within diverse groups.

Strategic team formation: Just as firefighters must quickly assemble and rely on various crew configurations based on who is available and what the situation demands, you can adopt a similar approach. By strategically forming teams to meet specific project needs or to address sudden market changes, you can leverage the best available talent. This might mean pulling together a cross-functional team to tackle a new client project or assembling a task force to address an unexpected challenge.

Emphasising flexibility and cross-training: To optimise dynamic team formations, it's crucial that employees are cross-trained and flexible. In firefighting, every team member understands the basics of each other's roles well enough to function cohesively under pressure. Similarly, in business, employees who have a broad understanding of different functions within the company can adapt more easily to varying team roles and responsibilities, enhancing the group's overall effectiveness.

Building trust quickly: One of the key challenges in rapidly changing team compositions is developing trust quickly among team members. Open communication, mutual respect, and shared goals become paramount. Regular team-building activities and open forums for sharing successes and challenges can accelerate team bonding.

Leveraging technology for coordination: Just as firefighters use apps and other communication tools to coordinate who responds to a call, you can use project management software and communication platforms to help manage team assignments and workflow. These tools can provide transparency about who is working on what and help teams coordinate efforts more efficiently, especially in fluid team arrangements.

Recognizing and rewarding adaptability: Every fireground operation will offer a new set of challenges and team configurations, just as business projects can vary in scope and requirements. Recognising and rewarding employees who demonstrate adaptability and perform well in various team settings through praise and awards can encourage a culture where flexibility is valued as a critical professional skill.

By adopting our crewing approach, you can create a versatile and responsive workforce capable of tackling a wide range of challenges.

When every situation is different, how you train your teams to respond will impact how well they will respond to the changes thrown at them. The more experienced they are, the less likely they are to react negatively to problems.

React or Respond?

When I was a new firefighter, like most people, I "reacted" to fire. That means that when I saw a fire, I would automatically go into action. I'd grab a hose and ask what I should do. After many years of experience, I've learnt that this is quite normal for anybody who's put into a stressful situation. But it's not necessarily the best way to deal with what's happening in front of you. When dealing with change, one of the first things you need to do is to stop, then assess the whole situation around you before you go into action. It's natural to react and to do anything to solve the problem as soon as possible, but that's not the best or the safest way to deal with any issue.

One of the senior firefighters in my brigade with a wealth of experience took me aside one day and told me a story. It was a story from when he was a young firefighter, and it sticks with me to this day. I tell it to every new firefighter that I train. This is what he told me:

"When I was a new firefighter in country New South Wales, we would often get fire calls, and like all fire brigades, we'd rush to the station, gear up, jump in a truck and turn out to the fire. Once we got to the fire, we would climb out and get ready to go into action, but the

Officer In Charge would stop us and tell us to stand by.

"Rather than just jumping out of the truck and instantly yelling commands, the Captain would take his time getting down. He'd stand beside the truck and get his 'rollies' out of his pocket. Being old school, he didn't smoke ready-made cigarettes; he liked to roll his own.

"As he stood there rolling a cigarette, he would look around and observe the fire. He'd take in what was happening. He didn't just send us in to start putting out the flames. He took one or two minutes to fully assess the situation before he made a decision. Once his cigarette was rolled and lit, he had collected enough information about what was going on in front of him, and that allowed him to form his fire action plan. It was then, and only then, that we would get our orders."

The funny thing is when I first heard this story, I could imagine this guy. When I was very young, my grandfather used to roll his own cigarettes, and I always remember watching him do it. I was always impressed by how he could do it whilst not looking down at his hands. Time stood still as I watched. Although it seemed to take quite a while, realistically it probably happened in less than a minute. When the picture of my grandfather and the Captain blended in my mind, it left an indelible impression on me.

I don't smoke, and I never have, but from this story I learnt that I needed to just get out of the truck and take my time to pull on my jacket, my helmet and my gloves. While I did that, I learned to look at what was going on around me and at the fire, so that I could make an informed plan about how we were going to go into action.

Sometimes you see things that need to be done immediately, like hitting the fire as it races up to the road's edge, threatening to jump over and up a hill where you might lose it for days. Decisions like that can be quickly implemented by the crew while I continue to look at the whole fire and form a plan. Other times when you're looking around, you'll see another fire in the distance that no one knows about yet. You need to call that into 000, so they can get crews on the road to start investigating while you're dealing with the fire in front of you. When *you see the bigger picture, you're in a better position mentally to make the right decisions.*

It took time to get better at stepping back and doing this. I had to overcome the urge to react. But it made me a better leader and a calmer leader when the pressure was on.

My mate's story did me the world of good not only on the fireground but also in my business, and I'll be forever grateful to the man who told it to me. There's an old saying that only fools rush in where angels fear to tread. I can't promise I'm an angel (I know my team are), but there's a lot of truth in the first part. When things change, you need to step back and stop. Take time to assess the situation properly and plan before you go into action. Only then, when you have a better idea of what is actually happening, not what appears to be happening, should you take action.

There have been times when I've had clients ring me in a blind panic fearing that something has happened to their website. After taking five minutes to ask some questions and do some quick checks, I'm in a better position to help them and to get the right outcome. What they think is happening is often not the case.

Whenever you're dealing with evolving situations, it's essential your team stops and assesses what's happening. When they don't, they're reacting to symptoms of the issue, not dealing with the cause or the possible results. Train them to think, then act.

Change-Proofing

"Fortify today with the wisdom of tomorrow, ensuring you're not just prepared for change but are paving its path to carry you to your goals."

Change-Proofing

Understanding that change is inevitable is a first step for any leader, but how you prepare for potential shifts can future-proof your organisation. Yes, you can respond to change as it happens, but the best leaders prepare their teams for what might happen long before it does.

As a firefighter, I'm always looking for ways to enhance our operational effectiveness. One recent upgrade is the integration of mapping software in our trucks, ensuring we always know our current location and our previous routes. This technology enhanced our efficiency and also bolstered crew safety.

Firefighting is continually evolving. We're currently experimenting with electric pumps and have introduced satellite receivers that enable global communication. Additionally, new lightweight uniforms are being trialled to provide better heat resistance during operations. Each advancement brings potential challenges that need addressing, yet they represent the forward momentum in our field. Staying informed about innovations in firefighting equips us with the knowledge to seamlessly integrate new tools and improve our systems.

While many of your daily tasks may remain constant over the years, aspects such as technology, external business conditions, and client expectations will undoubtedly change. Even if you can't foresee them all, it's essential to prepare yourself and your team for these possibilities. The processes and training you implement now will safeguard your organisation for the future, no matter what challenges arise.

Chapter 8:

The Imperative of Constant Vigilance

As a leader, you can never be complacent. Whether you're navigating a complex business deal or commanding a team on the fireground, alertness is crucial. Change is the only constant, and often, the shifts that impact us the most come with little warning and can escalate rapidly. In firefighting, we use the acronym LACES—Lookouts, Awareness, Communication, Escape Routes, and Safety—to maintain a continuous state of readiness on a fire. Each firefighter understands that it means to constantly look for change and danger, keep aware of what is happening near you, communicate to others what you're doing, where you're going and anything that you see changing, understand exactly which way to go to escape if the fire turns on us, and to make safety our priority.

This mantra is ingrained in every briefing and becomes second nature, ensuring everyone is always prepared, anticipatory, and responsive to the always evolving conditions.

This concept translates seamlessly into business management.

Staying informed about industry dynamics is not just about keeping up—it's about staying ahead. You must cultivate the habit of observing market trends, competitor moves, internal performance metrics, and broader economic indicators. It's about keeping your "head on a swivel", attentively scanning the environment for signs of change. Engage actively with your team, listen to industry chatter, analyse your data, and stay connected with the shifts in consumer behaviour.

Ignoring emerging issues or dismissing minor discrepancies can lead to significant crises that could have been mitigated or even avoided. Remember, in business as in firefighting, a small spark can quickly spread into a raging inferno. Leaders who fail to address these sparks are often those who watch their endeavours falter or fail. Being proactive, rather than reactive, sets the stage for sustained success and safety. Embrace a mindset of perpetual readiness, and empower your team to do the same, ensuring that when changes occur, your organisation is not just prepared to react, but poised to capitalise.

Throughout my time doing business online, I've worked with some of the largest multinational companies in the world and some of the smallest family businesses in my local area. They had one thing in common—none of them had a current backup of their website. It was a massive oversight on their part. A sizeable percentage of those websites were built using WordPress, a website content management system that is easy to use and ranks well in search engines.

As WordPress has become more popular, it has come to the attention of hackers. With over 72 million sites built on it, there is a significant opportunity for hackers to lock owners and their customers out of their websites. In some cases, this might not mean much if the site doesn't get much web traffic, but in others, it amounts to a loss of millions of dollars a day in lost sales and revenue.

As an SEO team, we weren't responsible for maintaining most of our clients' websites. Our job was to work with their teams to make the sites rank well and stay on top in Google search results. However, we always stressed the importance of keeping websites updated and taking regular backups. I knew from being a firefighter that the minute you take your eyes off what is going on around you, you set yourself up for failure. Despite our recommendations, many clients thought it couldn't happen to them.

Imagine my surprise when one of the largest companies in the world called me, about three years after our contract with them had ended, desperately asking if we might have a backup of their website. By habit, whenever we made changes, we took a local backup so that if anything went wrong, we could reload the site.

Luckily, on one of our encrypted offline backup storage systems, I was able to find an old but complete backup of their website. It turned out that the web team, which they paid a substantial amount of money to every month, didn't have any backups going back over three years!

Even though they had been informed that WordPress was a rich target for hackers, they had not been vigilant. All they needed to do was take two simple steps: set up an automated backup on their web server (it's built into the software) and download a copy monthly to store offline in case anything happened to the server. They could have easily set up the server to email a download link to them!

As a leader, regardless of your business, it's essential to stay alert to potential risks and take measures to mitigate them. Being prepared can prevent many issues from becoming disasters.

Preparation and Adaptability

In firefighting, as soon as we arrive at a fire, we assess the situation and formulate a plan. This involves establishing containment and fallback lines, integral for controlling the blaze. Just as a fire plan must be flexible to adapt to changing conditions, your business strategies must also be dynamic, allowing for adjustments in response to competitors, consumer demands, or internal challenges. It's vital to have contingency plans ready before the situation demands them, ensuring you're not caught off guard.

Your planning process should be thorough and well documented. We use SMEACS (Situation, Mission, Execution, Administration/ Logistics, Communication, and Safety), which is an incident planning and briefing aid to structure our fire attack plans. This can be equally relevant in a business context. By outlining each aspect of a project under these headings, every potential angle is considered. This methodical approach not only prepares teams for immediate tasks but also helps inculcate a mindset of readiness for unexpected developments.

Practical, scenario-based training forms the backbone of our preparedness. We might simulate fires using traffic cones or flashing lights in a training environment; you can adopt similar strategies by creating hypothetical scenarios that mimic real-world challenges. For instance, simulating a system outage or a critical project deadline can help teams practice navigating stress and troubleshooting under pressure. Changing variables during these simulations, such as introducing new problems or escalating existing ones, can enrich problem-solving skills.

Incorporating these real-world simulations in regular training schedules ensures that your teams don't just know their roles but are adept at adapting their strategies within those roles under pressure. This preparation is about making theoretical and practical knowledge second nature, allowing your teams to perform seamlessly when real challenges arise. Just as firefighters might need to find and fight a fire that isn't easily locatable, your teams might need to tackle problems that aren't immediately apparent.

Effective planning and robust training are about more than just preventing failures; they're about empowering teams to handle any situation confidently and competently. By adopting a comprehensive and flexible planning approach, and regularly assessing these plans against potential real-world challenges, leaders can forge teams that are skilled, knowledgeable, resilient and responsive to the dynamic landscapes in which they operate.

Example of a Simple SMEACS Briefing Form

SMEACS BRIEFING

Incident: ͨ	Operational Period — From: 1630 7.10.21 / To: 2030 7.10.21
Location:	
Prepared By: Brad Hauck	Date Prepared: 6.10.21
Position: 2nd Officer MRFB	Time Prepared:

PLANNING

Situation
Current situation

We are undertaking a HR burn to assist local land owner clear out a small parcel of unburnt bushland next to our completed Monaro Rd Burn from earlier this year.

Mission
Define incident control objectives

To complete a low intensity, mosaic burn to area of bush at the back of

Execution
How control of incident will be achieved. Tactics that will be implemented

M52 will be situated at ALPHA on the driveway of 16 Manuka Rd to provide protection of the top side of the fire.
M51 will be situated at BRAVO in   I to cover the side of the burn.
M41 will be situated at CHARLIE in   I to cover the side of the burn up to M52.
The burn will be conducted from M52 corner down to   I using a range of lighting techniques to provide max control over the fire and a cool burn.

Administration
Logistical arrangements

Crews will meet at station to leave at 1630. Some PVs will be needed.

Command and Communications
Command structure and reporting system. Maintenance of communication.

Communications will be via GWN. TAC channel to be advised or 859. Mudgee 2 will be Incident Controller.

Safety
Safety issues.

Watch out for slips, trips and falls. This burn is on a hill so move carefully. Wear full PPE and follow standard COVID protocols. Stay hydrated.

Time of Briefing:	Briefing to:	Person's Names:
	Unit	Mudgeeraba Rural Fire Brigade
	Division	
	Sector	

Embracing Change: The Key to Dynamic Leadership

Being open to change is not just an option for today's leaders; it's a necessity. Leaders must cultivate an environment where adaptability is embraced, not just by themselves but by every team member. It's not about discarding tried-and-tested procedures but about being ready to evolve them as circumstances demand. Understanding your team's dynamics is crucial. Identify those who are eager to grow and can champion change within the organisation. These are the individuals who see potential where others see obstacles, and their enthusiasm can be infectious, helping to motivate others to embrace new challenges.

Leadership involves more than guiding operations; it's about inspiring your team to see change as an opportunity for growth. This mindset should be encouraged across all levels of your team, even if it means making tough decisions about personnel who may not adapt well. Creating a safe space for open dialogue is essential. Encourage your team to share ideas and feedback freely. Remember, great ideas often come from collaborative brainstorming, where diverse experiences and viewpoints can intersect to produce innovative solutions.

Celebrating Flexibility: Recognizing Adaptive Success

In any dynamic environment, flexibility is a trait worth celebrating. Acknowledging and praising team members who adapt well to new situations encourages others to embrace change. This doesn't require grand gestures; simple affirmations for small achievements can significantly boost morale. For instance, recognising someone for successfully handling a challenging phone call or navigating a new task can reinforce their confidence and willingness to engage with change.

Understanding the individual capabilities within your team is crucial. Some members may naturally thrive in shifting environments, while others might struggle and need more support and encouragement. Tailor your support and recognise efforts at every level. Encourage your team leaders to do the same, creating a culture where flexibility is valued, and adaptation is viewed as a skill to be developed.

By fostering a workplace that supports continuous learning, you can build teams that are not just equipped to handle change but proactively seek it. This kind of environment not only leads to future-proofed, resilient and innovative teams but also ensures that the organisation as a whole can respond fluidly to the demands of the market and the needs of its clients.

Future-Proofing Leadership through Adaptability and Resilience

Effective leadership is synonymous with adaptability and preparedness. In this chapter I've stressed the importance of being ready for anything, making robust but flexible plans, embracing change, and fostering a culture that not only tolerates but celebrates elasticity.

You must remain vigilant, always on the lookout for signs of change that could affect your team or business. You need to cultivate an environment where plans are dynamic and can be adapted swiftly in response to new challenges. Regular training and preparedness exercises ensure you're your teams do not become complacent, instead equipping them with the skills needed to respond effectively to emergencies and routine changes alike.

Future-proofing leadership means building a foundation of trust, fostering open communication, and ensuring that every team member feels capable, valued and understood. Leaders who invest in these areas will create resilient teams that can withstand and thrive in the face of change, displaying robustness and adaptability in a rapidly evolving environment.

After a morning spent containing a significant wildfire, we returned to the Incident Control Centre (ICC), reflecting on the severe drought conditions that heightened the fire threat. We barely had time to start our lunch when the Operations Officer urgently informed us, "The fire has flared up near the road about 1–2 km away. Can you go and extinguish it ASAP before it jumps to the unburnt side?"

Immediately, we re-equipped and raced to the flare-up. On arrival, we positioned the truck strategically, allowing quick access to the hose reels while keeping the truck protected. With strong winds challenging our efforts and a new recruit by my side, I led the initial attack to demonstrate effective firefighting techniques, quickly handing over to the recruit for him to finish extinguishing the spot fire.

The situation escalated when we received a distress call from a light attack vehicle engaged nearby. Upon arrival, we discovered the fire had breached the containment line, posing an imminent threat to other crews trapped in the "Dead Man's Zone", an area at high risk of burning within five minutes under current wind conditions. We advised the light attack crew to evacuate and engaged the new fire front, which was rapidly spreading.

As the fire grew uncontrollable and the winds intensified, I made the decision to retreat and prioritise my crew's safety. The fire was now too big and too fast moving to be stopped, leading to our strategic withdrawal to a main road to keep the fire from crossing. Following our withdrawal, other crews fell back to a containment line 3 km in front of the fire and successfully implemented a backburn to contain the fire moving towards them.

This day again highlighted the critical importance of adaptability. Our initial efforts might have seemed in vain, but by quickly adjusting to escalating conditions and modifying our strategy, ultimately, we succeeded.

The Incident Commander's prior preparation and planning of fallback lines not only ensured the safety of our crews but also contributed significantly to the containment of the fire. Being prepared *for potential changes made all the difference to our success. This experience also provided a crucial, real-life learning opportunity for the new recruit—plus we got to celebrate with ice cream on the way back to the station.*

What You Can do Prepare for Change

To integrate the concepts of embracing change and praising flexibility into your leadership and organizational culture, consider implementing these steps:

Conduct Regular Change Readiness Assessments

Regularly evaluate how well your team or organization is equipped to handle change. This can involve surveys, meetings, or informal check-ins that help you gauge the team's current state of readiness and to pinpoint areas that may need more support or resources.

Implement Adaptive Training Programs

Develop training sessions that focus not only on skills necessary for current tasks but also for potential changes. Include scenario-based learning that mimics real-world challenges, encouraging team members to think on their feet and adapt quickly.

Foster an Open Communication Environment

Create and maintain an environment where team members feel safe to express their ideas, concerns, and suggestions without fear of ridicule or retribution. This could be facilitated through regular team meetings, suggestion boxes, or open-door policy days.

Recognise and Reward Flexibility

Actively look for and publicly praise instances of team members adapting well to changes, no matter how small. This recognition can be as simple as verbal praise, notes of appreciation, or small rewards that acknowledge their efforts.

Cultivate Peer Support Networks

Encourage the formation of peer support networks within your team where more adaptable members can help others who may struggle with change. Peer mentoring can be an effective way to spread adaptive skills and strengthen team bonds.

By taking these steps, leaders can ensure that their teams are not only prepared to handle change but can also thrive in changing environments. These actions will help build a resilient, flexible, and innovative team that views change as an opportunity for growth and improvement.

For a downloadable version of this "Action Plan for Future & Change-Proofing Your Business", please visit my website: *FirefighterBrad.com/bookresources.*

Training Exercise: Adaptive Readiness Simulation

Objective: To assess and enhance the team's readiness to adapt to sudden changes in the business environment, using principles from firefighting strategies like LACES and SMEACS.

Materials Needed:

- Scenario descriptions (prepared in advance)
- Role assignment cards
- Timers
- Feedback forms
- Incident Planning and Briefing Aid (SMEACS form)

Exercise Overview: This simulation exercise will involve a series of rapid, unexpected changes to test how well teams can adapt using predefined strategies. The exercise mimics real-world business disruptions, ranging from market shifts and technological failures to key personnel losses.

Steps:

1. **Preparation:**
   - Divide participants into teams.
   - Assign roles to each member (e.g., Team Leader, Communications Officer, Logistics Coordinator).
   - Provide a brief overview of what the acronyms LACES and SMEAC mean.

2. **Initial Briefing:**
   - Present the teams with an initial business scenario that is running smoothly.
   - Teams use the SMEACS form to plan their approach.

3. Scenario Change Introduction:

- Introduce sudden changes to the scenario (e.g., a major product flaw is discovered, a key supplier goes bankrupt).

- Teams must quickly reassess and adjust their strategies.

4. Role Play:

- Teams enact their roles, making decisions based on the evolving scenario.

- Facilitators introduce additional changes or complications at timed intervals.

5. Use of LACES:

- Throughout the exercise, remind teams to apply the LACES principles:

  - **Lookouts:** Maintain awareness of further external changes.

  - **Awareness:** Keep track of internal team dynamics and resources.

  - **Communication:** Ensure clear and continuous communication within the team and with external stakeholders.

  - **Escape routes:** Plan for worst-case scenarios.

  - **Safety:** Prioritize the team and company's long-term health.

6. Debriefing:

- Teams discuss what strategies worked, what didn't, and how they adapted to each new challenge.

- Feedback is shared among groups to foster learning

and improvement.

7. Feedback and Reflection:

- Participants fill out feedback forms based on their experiences.

- Discuss the importance of adaptability and contingency planning in business continuity.

8. Follow-Up:

- Provide additional resources on adaptive strategies in business.

- Plan follow-up sessions to reinforce lessons learned and introduce new adaptation techniques.

Learning Outcomes:

- Enhanced ability to quickly adapt to and plan for unexpected changes.

- Improved team communication and role flexibility.

- Greater understanding of applying strategic firefighting principles like LACES and SMEACS in business contexts.

This exercise not only prepares teams to handle unforeseen business challenges but also emphasizes the importance of continuous vigilance and readiness, drawing parallels between firefighting preparedness and business adaptability.

Chapter 9:

Upskill Now, Not Later

Embracing technology is essential if you aim to change-proof your team and stay ahead of the curve. Industry-specific email newsletters, podcasts, YouTube channels, and topic alerts can keep you informed and prepared for the next big thing. Don't allow outdated technology or software to stifle your organisation's growth. Experiment with new software, test emerging AI tools, and stay engaged with the latest developments. Keep an eye out for technological advancements that can elevate your team's performance and ensure your operations are as effective and cutting-edge as possible. For those keen to delve deeper, consider joining specialized forums or groups, like my "Marketing with AI and ChatGPT" Facebook group, where updates, tips and discussions can provide valuable insights.

At industry conferences, make a point to visit technology tables to discover what tools different sectors are utilising. Often, these tools are not yet widespread in your own country, presenting an opportunity to pioneer their adoption within your local market. As firefighters, we approach new tools with an open mind but always test them in controlled, non-critical environments first. This ensures that any new technology is both effective and safe for use, whether on the fireground or in the office.

It's crucial that everyone on your team is proficient with the latest technology that impacts your field. Encourage team members to explore tech that aligns with their professional skills and personal interests. This approach helps them quickly discern the advantages and limitations of new tools. Facilitate sessions where they can share their findings and lead training on beneficial technologies. This not only enhances skills but also fosters a culture of continuous learning and knowledge sharing.

Promote an environment of "unrestricted play". Allow team members the freedom to experiment with new technologies in their own way. This unstructured exploration is vital for genuine understanding and innovative applications in your workflows. Pre-emptive adoption and adaptation of new technologies before external pressures demand change can significantly empower your team, keeping you well prepared and ahead of competitors.

Remember, technology in this context isn't limited to digital tools. It includes any equipment that can enhance efficiency, from advanced computing solutions to simpler hardware upgrades like more efficient hammers or enhanced battery drills. As a leader, you must leverage every tool available to boost productivity, profitability, and success rates.

10 Key Rules for Technology Upskilling

Here are my 10 key strategies for ensuring new technology is managed and prioritised in any organisation.

1. Stay informed with digital tools: Utilise email newsletters, podcasts, YouTube, and topic alerts to stay ahead of industry trends.

2. Experiment with new technologies: Regularly test new software and AI tools to determine their applicability and potential benefit to your business.

3. Engage in tech communities: Join forums and groups, like the Marketing with AI and ChatGPT Facebook group, for regular updates and discussions on the latest technologies.

4. Explore at conferences: Visit technology exhibits at conferences to discover tools that could be implemented in your business, potentially even before they become widely available in your market.

5. Undertake controlled testing: Introduce new technologies in safe, non-critical environments to assess their effectiveness and safety before full-scale implementation.

6. Educate our teams: Ensure all team members are trained and comfortable with new technologies that impact your field.

7. Lead through learning: Encourage team members with specific skills or interests in technology to explore new tools and lead training sessions.

8. Promote unrestricted exploration: Allow team members time and freedom to experiment with new technologies in their own way to foster understanding and innovation.

9. Think beyond digital: Consider all forms of technology that can improve efficiency, from software upgrades to hardware enhancements like better tools and equipment.

10.   Seek continuous improvement: Always be on the lookout for technological advancements that can enhance productivity, profitability, and success.

Create A Superior Mindset

Encourage "New Ideas" Thinking

Leaders' minds are perpetually ticking. For example, upon discovering a new software program that could help with operations or something as simple as a set of storage drawers, I immediately think about how these might be utilised in the fire station, or alternatively, in my own business. This constant quest for innovation should be a core trait in any leader. Innovation not only helps you become a market leader, but it also ensures that you're ahead of change before it happens.

I encourage you to instil this mindset in your team. By nurturing an environment where everyone is keen to suggest improvements and new ideas, you are future-proofing your operations. Remember, the collective insight of your team is invariably richer than relying on a single perspective—especially when it's your own.

Foster a culture where sharing and speaking up is not just encouraged but automatic. This will keep your team ahead of the curve, constantly innovating and adapting.

Institute a Personal Learning and Development Plan

The path to change-proofing yourself and your people has to involve constant personal growth and development. Just like your team, you need to be engaging regularly with books, podcasts, and videos, attending conferences and networking with other leaders to exchange ideas and strategies. However, remember that your health and physical development is just as crucial as your knowledge. Maintain physical fitness, eat well, and ensure you get enough rest. Mental resilience is also critical; practise daily meditation to manage stress effectively. It's important to not only debrief others after a stressful incident but to seek debriefing yourself, perhaps with a mentor or a trusted peer. Taking regular breaks to recharge is essential; if you're leading effectively, your team will easily handle responsibilities in your absence.

Develop a Collective Learning Environment

Learning isn't passive—it requires creating opportunities for active engagement. Set up mentoring programs and encourage team collaboration to allow both you and your team members to learn from each other's successes and mistakes. Organise team activities like first aid courses, which, while they may start with mundane theory, often end with enjoyable practical exercises that enhance team bonding. These shared experiences not only educate but also integrate new members into the team culture, preparing them to back each other when times are tough.

Embrace and Implement Useful Feedback

Feedback sucks. There, I've said it. No one likes to hear how they're going unless it's positive. We all dread hearing what we're doing wrong. But if we are going to change-proof our teams, then we need to encourage them to embrace feedback because that's one of the main improvement mechanisms we have.

For a team to truly embrace change and improve, feedback must be understood as being a valuable tool. Your team needs to learn how to deliver and receive feedback constructively. Structure debriefs to address what worked, what didn't, and what could be improved, without focusing on blame. Private sessions with a mentor can be particularly beneficial for leaders, providing a safe space for you and your leaders to reflect on your actions and receive targeted advice.

Learning *how* to give feedback is key. You can talk about the failures without being negative. Sometimes just telling someone something honestly allows them to see where they can get better.

When I first volunteered for the role of Divisional Commander, I believed I was prepared for the responsibilities it entailed despite lacking formal training in the area. However, after recently completing a relevant course, I've come to realise the extent of the mistakes I made during my initial shift.

That day, I had dispatched my crews and sector commanders to their respective sectors, and they were performing excellently. However, we encountered severe communication issues due to unreliable radio comms, making it difficult to maintain contact and convey messages effectively.

As the shift was winding down, I sent two crews to check one of the sector containment lines one last time. I thought I had made it clear to do a quick inspection and then return to their stations (Code 4). Initially, I received a report that all was well, and since there were no further tasks, I released the remaining crews and awaited confirmation from the two tasked crews. After an hour without any communication, and unable to reach them either in person or via radio, I made a critical error. I assumed they had returned safely and simply hadn't managed to contact me due to the ongoing radio problems. Consequently, I closed the Division and went home.

The following day, I received a call from the Operations Officer informing me that I had inadvertently left crews on the fireground. They had been delayed by a hazardous tree near the containment line and were unable to reach out for assistance. Understandably, they were upset—a sentiment I empathised with deeply, having been in similar situations myself. I apologised profusely to the Ops Officer and explained the circumstances. He was understanding but made it crystal clear that such oversights were unacceptable, which I took to heart.

Horrified by my oversight, I revisited my notes from the shift for contact details and called both Crew Leaders to apologise personally. One accepted my apology during our conversation, expressing their frustration but acknowledging the situation. The other was not available, so I left a message, hoping they would understand.

Being criticised by someone I deeply respected was painful. The feedback highlighted my failure and the disappointment it caused. This experience has been indelibly etched into my memory, and I am committed to never repeating this mistake. Such moments are harsh but valuable, shaping us into more capable and conscientious leaders. At the time, my failure cut deeply, but the feedback has made me a better firefighter. Being able to accept feedback will make you a better leader.

Keep Safe and Compliant

Maintaining rigorous safety standards is not just a "government" requirement; it's a foundation of workplace culture that spans from firefighting to corporate environments. By implementing routine debriefings after each project or operational activity, you can ensure ongoing improvement and compliance with safety protocols.

This approach doesn't just uphold existing safety standards—it also focuses the team's ability to anticipate and adapt to future challenges, increasing efficiency and effectiveness in handling those situations if they happen again. Continuously improving safety measures means that safety becomes a natural part of your daily workflow, rather than just a checklist item.

A safe workplace benefits everyone, now and in the future. On the fireground, safety allows crew members to tackle more challenging tasks. This is because a controlled, safe environment removes distractions and fears, enabling everyone to focus entirely on the task at hand with confidence.

Safety practices significantly impact overall workplace well-being. They help prevent accidents and injuries, which is critical for minimising downtime and reducing ongoing operational costs. Robust safety training and protocols boost morale and productivity by creating a secure and trustful work environment.

Additionally, a strong safety culture is crucial for maintaining a positive reputation. It demonstrates a commitment to team welfare and operational excellence, strengthening client confidence. Compliance with legal and regulatory requirements also protects you from potential legal consequences and fines.

Fostering this kind of safety-oriented culture distinguishes high-performing leaders from their less vigilant counterparts.

Remember, safety first!

Commit to Upskilling

The significance of upskilling yourself and your team in all areas cannot be overstated, particularly in fields as dynamic and demanding as firefighting. To truly future-proof your team, it's crucial that they enhance their technological proficiency, embark on personal development, engage in collective learning, and adopt a positive attitude towards feedback. Additionally, ensuring that upskilling includes a focus on safety and compliance is critical to maintaining high standards and readiness for any challenge that gets thrown at you.

At our station, the responsibility of progressing towards the future of firefighting is shared by everyone. We operate on the principle that if one team member acquires a new and useful skill, it's their duty to help elevate the entire team. This culture of shared growth enhances individual capabilities and also strengthens our collective performance.

A leader must set an expectation that everyone will contribute to the continuous improvement of your team. Doing so ensures that while your team becomes more proficient with new technologies and methods, they are also up to date with the latest safety protocols and legal requirements, which are just as vital.

You need to seek out opportunities for training and development, encouraging team members to pursue learning, and facilitating the sharing of knowledge across all levels. This means that the entire organization keeps pace with the evolving business landscape and is also prepared to handle future challenges with competence, confidence, and a strong adherence to safety standards.

Remember, a team that learns together grows together. Lead by example and expect the same commitment to advancement and compliance from your team!

Chapter 10:

Preparation, Responsiveness, and Strength

Embracing a proactive approach to change-proofing is essential, whether you're a firefighter awaiting the next alarm or a leader in a fast-paced business environment. We firefighters are trained extensively on procedural steps long before encountering our first real flames. Skills like reading a page sent by Firecom, navigating to incidents, gearing up or preparing a truck for deployment are all rehearsed rigorously to ingrain the process and the thinking behind them. This structured readiness ensures that once on the scene, our minds and actions are already in sync with the demands of the situation.

In the business world, this principle equally holds true. Upon receiving a task, whether it comes through a call or an email, the preparation should begin immediately. This could involve drafting a brief, assembling the right team, or pulling together necessary resources. Establishing clear, repeatable processes within your team enhances efficiency, builds confidence, and reduces hesitation or fear in action.

Firefighters train not just until they get it right but until they cannot get it wrong. This philosophy should permeate your practices as well. Implementing standard operating procedures and checklists can mitigate fear and inertia, allowing common problems to be addressed systematically and efficiently. Don't wait. Start now to refine the processes which will enable you and your team to act swiftly and effectively, prepared for changes as they arise.

During the challenging 2019/2020 Black Summer fire season, our conventional firefighting approaches were often insufficient. We faced continuous, unpredictable crises which reinforced the need to be adaptable and resilient. The adage "It is what it is", frequently uttered by my colleague Wayne, encapsulated this mindset—acknowledging that despite our best efforts, some factors remain well beyond our control.

Like firefighters who train meticulously for emergencies, you should prepare rigorously for industry shifts and challenges. Establishing simple protocols for rapid response not only streamlines your operations but also equips your teams with the confidence to handle high-pressure situations efficiently.

Having procedures in place ensures that when a business challenge arises, your response is swift and decisive, mirroring a firefighter's instinctual reaction to each new development. This level of preparedness will help you build a resilient culture, capable of adapting quickly to change and overcoming obstacles with precision and determination. Things will never flow as smoothly as you expect.

As a keynote speaker, I get asked to speak about leadership all over the world. Standing on a stage in front of 500 people, with all those eyes on you and everyone hoping to learn something that will positively change their life or business, can be daunting. But I love it. However, getting up on stage requires a lot of preparation.

If I have to deliver a 45-minute speech, I will practise it a minimum of ten times before I get anywhere near the stage. While I don't memorise it word for word, my simple photographic slides help jog my memory instantly. Normally, everything goes well, and I enjoy myself, but things don't always go perfectly.

One time, I was invited to speak in another state. I wrote and practised my speech for about a month leading up to the engagement. I had always done this, not just because I wanted to know my speech but because my firefighter training had taught me do things until I couldn't do them wrong when I was under pressure.

The day before I was due on stage, I headed to the airport and flew down. I arrived at my hotel and settled into my room when suddenly it hit me—the worst flu I've ever had. I'm not sure how or when I caught it, but I got next to zero sleep that night. It was a very long night.

When the sun rose the next morning, I forced myself out of bed, ate, and got ready for my speech. I was expected on stage, and although I knew I could have informed the organizers that I wasn't well, I felt a responsibility to those who had come a long way to hear me. I took a couple of Panadol and headed to the auditorium, keeping myself distanced from everyone else.

I don't remember much of that speech, but I do recall flashes of people clapping at the end and coming up to tell me they had really enjoyed my message. Some even approached me years later at other venues, saying how much they had enjoyed that speech and how they were ready to take lots of notes again.

All my preparation and practice saved me on that day. If I hadn't taken the time and effort to get to know my speech, there is no possible way I could have successfully delivered it in that condition. I've spoken on many stages since then, but thankfully, I've never been that sick again. This experience reinforced for me the importance of preparedness—it's what enables us to perform even when circumstances are far from ideal.

Mixing Planning with Action

The urgency of firefighting taught me the importance of timely decision-making. Initially, I stop, make a quick assessment and establish a plan of attack, which can be adapted as the situation evolves. This method applies to any high-pressure scenario in business or emergency response. It's crucial to prioritise effectively, considering the welfare of people, property, and the environment in that order.

However, it's vital to separate planning from execution to avoid hasty reactions that can lead to oversight and errors. Effective leaders stop or pause to evaluate the situation thoroughly before acting. This approach prevents the chaos of reacting without a strategy, which not only compounds problems but also undermines a leader's credibility. Reacting rather than responding often leads to failure.

By adhering to these principles, you can not only respond to immediate challenges but also foster a culture of preparedness and adaptability within your team that stands up to the test of rapid and relentless change.

Get Stronger

To lead your team through periods of rapid change, it's crucial to foster resilience well in advance—before you're facing a crisis. Just as firefighters rigorously train for emergencies, they also focus on physical fitness, proper nutrition, hydration, and mental health. This ensures they're ready to handle high-pressure situations. You need to adopt a similar approach. Your experience and training will equip you with a broad set of skills and the necessary knowledge to remain adaptable under any circumstances. Ensuring you and your team engage in healthy habits strengthens your mental fortitude and helps future-proof everyone for potential challenges. Remember, your team members are future leaders who will need to stand firm when situations deteriorate. Building adaptability and resilience is an ongoing process, reflecting the cyclical nature of crises, with each presenting a range of unique and escalating challenges.

Getting Good at Changing

I pride myself on being able to adapt quickly and efficiently, though I admit, some changes are harder to accept than others. For instance, I'm agile and responsive on the fireground, yet I find myself frustrated when a flight is delayed. This frustration stems from a human preference for predictability and control over our environment. Recognising when you can influence change and when to simply roll with it can significantly reduce stress. Embracing the "It is what it is" philosophy has helped me accept situations beyond my control, strengthening my resilience and helping me manage change better. When things get really tough, it enables me to accept things that I can't change and move forward positively!

Sticking Together

Navigating through change is considerably easier with a supportive team by your side. A cohesive team not only stands with you during change but also excels and grows through these experiences. By acknowledging and praising your team's efforts, especially in times of change, you reinforce their value and foster a positive, collaborative environment. My background as an only child and a swimmer taught me the value of independence, yet it was through my involvement in community organisations like Scouting and the Rural Fire Service Queensland (RFSQ) that I properly appreciated the power of collective effort.

Working towards a common goal enhances the satisfaction of the entire team. Winning alone is rewarding, but achieving success as a team offers a profound sense of collective accomplishment. This team spirit is vital, especially in critical times, allowing you to know exactly who to rely on for various challenges. While it's essential to offer opportunities to newcomers, in urgent situations, knowing your team's strengths can be invaluable.

In our brigade, fire trucks are equipped with everything necessary, whether it's a local call or a week-long deployment. This comprehensive set-up enables us to tackle nearly any situation and contain fires effectively.

However, we can't assume that all the required equipment is on board. That's why one of the essential skills we teach to new recruits is how to conduct a truck check. Using a checklist accessible on their phones, recruits meticulously inspect every locker, storage bin, and the cabin. If anything is missing, they must replace it from our spares or notify the officer responsible for truck maintenance. It's imperative that any missing item is replaced as soon as possible.

With practice, these checks become second nature. Experienced firefighters like me can assess what's missing with just a glance and complete the process in under five minutes. This efficiency is crucial; we need to trust that everything is in place when we respond urgently to a fire. Discovering missing tools, adapters, or hoses in such moments can be incredibly frustrating.

Upon returning from a fire call, our first task is to reset the truck. This involves washing dirty hoses, refilling tanks, topping up drinking water and foam, and cleaning everything thoroughly to ensure the truck is ready for immediate redeployment. This routine is vital. I recall days when, after resetting the truck, we were turned out to another fire call multiple times.

Truck checks might seem mundane, but they are fundamentally important. They ensure that when circumstances change and I need to adapt my tactics quickly, I can rely on finding what I need in the truck. This readiness to respond at any time and handle whatever comes our way is not just about being prepared; it represents the strength and resilience of our brigade. To me, a well-maintained truck symbolises our commitment to preparation, responsiveness, and the strength to face future challenges. It's at the heart of how we future-proof our operations.

Preparation = Success

In wrapping up this section on change-proofing, we've looked at how staying alert and adaptable isn't about keeping up—it's about leading the way. Whether we're talking about battling wildfires or navigating your businesses challenges, the key takeaway is the same: embrace change as a constant. Think of it as staying ahead of the curve, where using your initiative isn't just a strategy, but a mindset that turns potential disruptions into opportunities. It's about seeing beyond the immediate challenges and setting the stage for your continued success. By fostering this mindset, you don't just react to change; you anticipate it, you harness it, and you thrive in it. This approach doesn't just safeguard your present; it actively shapes your future, ensuring you're always ready, no matter what's ahead.

Embracing this philosophy means recognising that change is not a hurdle but a stepping stone to innovation and growth. In the firefighting world, it might mean adopting new technologies or strategies that enhance safety and effectiveness, long before they become industry standards or are even accepted as possible. In business, it involves continuously scanning the horizon for emerging trends and client shifts, ready to pivot your strategies at a moment's notice. This level of vigilance and flexibility can transform potential threats into powerful catalysts for improvement.

Instilling this adaptive approach within your team cultivates an environment rich in resilience and creativity. It encourages everyone to contribute their insights and ideas, creating a collective mastermind that is far greater than the sum of its parts. Teams that are encouraged to think flexibly and react adaptively are not only better equipped to handle changes but are also more engaged and invested in their roles. They see themselves as active participants in the business's growth, empowered to influence outcomes and drive each other's success.

Change-proofing is much more than a defensive tactic; it's an offensive strategy that empowers you as a leader and your team to not just survive but actually excel in an unpredictable world. By embracing change as an inevitable and beneficial aspect of our professional lives, we open the door to endless possibilities. Don't just adapt to change; let's anticipate it, welcome it, and use it to propel us forward. This is what sets apart true leaders from mere managers, marking the path not only for survival but for a thriving, dynamic future.

Chapter 11:

Your Change-Embracing Legacy

As you reach the end of this book, I hope you've gained a new appreciation for the powerful parallels between the discipline of firefighting and effective business leadership when dealing with rapid change. Throughout these chapters, I've explored how the mindset, strategies, and skills I honed on the fireground can serve as an practical blueprint for navigating the ever-changing environment of your leadership journey.

Yet, this book is about more than just a collection of stories and thoughts. It's a call to action. The principles and lessons I've shared are not meant to be merely studied but rather internalised and put into practice by you. Why? Because the true mark of a leader is not just your ability to manage the day to day, but your capacity to future-proof your organisation, your team, and yourself. When change hits you like a wildfire, you'll be ready!

I want to leave you with a final set of reflections and recommendations to help you cement your legacy as a change-proofed leader—one who not only survives the flames of change, but one who harnesses them to drive innovation, growth, and success.

Embrace the Inevitability of Change

The first and most fundamental step in becoming an agile leader is to fully embrace the inevitability of change.

Change is not something to be feared or resisted—it is a constant force that shapes our progress and defines our capacity to shine under pressure. As a leader, your ability to anticipate, adapt, and even instigate change will be the key difference between thriving and merely surviving.

This mindset shift can be challenging, especially when you have found comfort and success in the status quo. But the sooner you come to terms with the fact that change is not only unavoidable but essential, the better equipped you'll be to lead through the firestorms of the future.

Cultivate a Culture of Adaptability

With a change-embracing mindset in place, the next step is to foster a culture of adaptability within your team. Actively create an environment where flexibility, agility, and a willingness to experiment are not just encouraged, but rewarded.

For inspiration, look to the way we manage our crewing at fires. Just as firefighters must be prepared to work with different team members on every call, your business should be structured to enable seamless transitions and collaborative problem-solving, regardless of who is on your team.

Empower your team members to take on new roles, cross-train in unfamiliar teams, and bring their refreshed perspectives to the table. Celebrate those who face their fears, show courage to step out of their comfort zones and adapt to changing circumstances. By doing so, you'll not only make your organisation more resilient, but you'll also build a culture of innovation that will help you win in the years to come.

Implement a Strategy of Preparedness

You realise by now that fostering adaptability is only one piece of a bigger puzzle. True leadership also requires meticulous preparation and a commitment to ongoing learning and skill development.

Again, you can draw valuable lessons from my firefighting experience. Rigorous, regularly scheduled training sessions, detailed contingency planning, and a steadfast dedication to maintaining equipment and systems are all hallmarks of a properly prepared fire brigade. These principles can, and should, be applied to your business as well.

Establish comprehensive training programs that go beyond just imparting technical knowledge. Incorporate scenario-based exercises that challenge your team to think on their feet and adapt to rapidly evolving situations. Break their locked-in habits! Implement a thorough debriefing processes that allows you and them to learn from both successes and failures, continuously refining your strategies and procedures.

Don't limit your preparedness efforts to your internal operations. Stay alert to industry trends, competitor moves, and shifting client needs. Take the time to grow a diverse network of peers and mentors who can provide valuable insights and alternative perspectives. By keeping your finger on the pulse of your broader environment, you'll be better equipped to anticipate and respond to external changes long before they catch you off guard.

Leverage Technology for Adaptability

In today's digital world, the effective integration of technology is critical. While it's easy to get caught up in the latest tech trends, the true power of technology lies in its ability to enhance your organisation's adaptability and responsiveness. Remember, technology refers to all tools, not just software and hardware as so many people tend to think.

Look to the firefighting community's approach to new tools and equipment for inspiration. Rather than blindly adopting the newest gadgets, we rigorously test and evaluate new technologies in controlled environments before rolling them out in the field. This measured approach should be the foundation of your own technology integration strategy.

Encourage your team to experiment with emerging tools and platforms, but provide the guidance and resources necessary to ensure they are leveraged in a way that aligns with your mission. Empower tech-savvy team members to share their expertise, teaching their colleagues how to maximise the benefits of these new capabilities.

As mentioned earlier, don't limit your technological focus to just digital solutions. Consider how advancements in physical tools, equipment, and infrastructure can also enhance your adaptability and resilience. The agile leader looks holistically at the role of technology in driving progress, not just across software and systems, but throughout the entire operational landscape.

Cultivate a Mindset of Continuous Growth

The key to change-proof leadership lies not just in the strategies and tactics you employ, but in the mindset you cultivate—both within yourself and throughout your team.

The most effective leaders are those who embrace a mindset of continuous growth and improvement, always seeking to expand their knowledge, sharpen their skills, and challenge their own thinking. They understand that complacency is the enemy of progress, and that the day they stop learning is the day they stop being real leaders.

Foster this mindset by making personal development a priority, not just for yourself but for your entire team. Encourage ongoing education, whether through formal training programs, industry events, or simply setting aside time for team members to explore new ideas and share their new knowledge. Create a respectful culture in which seeking feedback and admitting mistakes are seen not as weaknesses but as opportunities for growth and advancement.

Most importantly, lead by example. Demonstrate your own commitment to continuous learning and adaptability, and your team will be inspired to follow suit. When they see you embracing change, taking risks, and pushing the boundaries of what's possible, they'll be empowered to do the same.

Create Your Legacy

As you continue on your journey of leadership, I urge you to remember that your legacy will not be defined by what you've overcome, but by the leaders you've helped to discover and build. Why? Because in the end, the true mark of your leadership is not just your own resilience and adaptability, but your ability to embed those qualities in the people you lead.

Think back to the fire crews I've talked about throughout this book—the ones who displayed unwavering courage, quick thinking, and a steadfast commitment to the mission, no matter the obstacles they faced. These are my mates who inspire me, not just for their personal success, but for the way they've lifted up their teams, empowered each other, and elevated the entire firefighting community.

This is the legacy I encourage you to strive for, too. By building a future-proof business filled with adaptable, resilient, and growth-minded people, you'll create a lasting impact that extends far beyond your own time there. Your team will be better equipped to navigate the challenges of tomorrow, the business will be positioned to thrive in the face of change, and your own leadership will be remembered not just for its effectiveness, but for its transformative power.

So, as you close this book and you prepare to embark on the next chapter of your journey, I challenge you to embrace the future-proof mindset with unwavering commitment. Be a leader who doesn't just react to change but responds to it and proactively shapes it. Be a leader who doesn't just manage the present but forges the path to a more resilient, innovative, and flame-proof tomorrow.

The road ahead may be uncertain, but with the lessons and principles we've discussed here, I have no doubt that you will find the courage, the creativity, and the competence to lead your organisation and your people to new heights of success. So, go forth—and remember, run towards the flames!

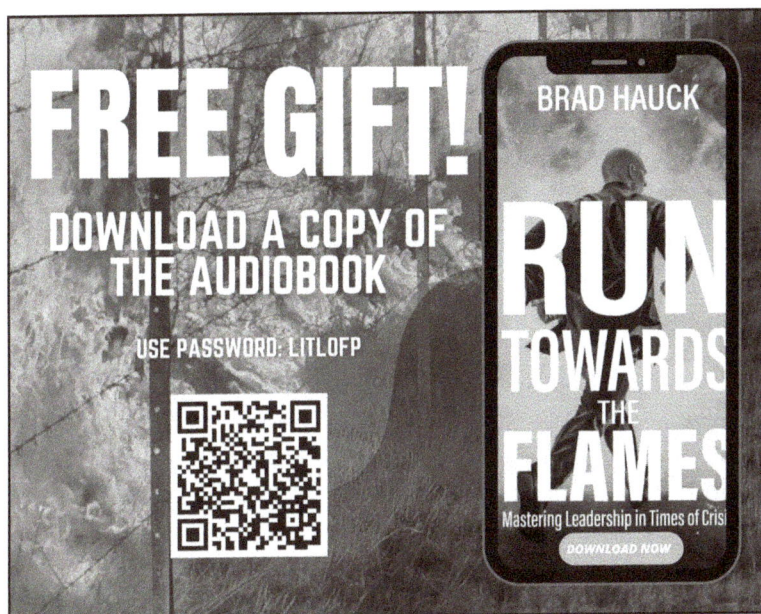

FREE AUDIO BOOK

To my Favourite Reader,

I'd like to thank you for reading Run Towards The Flames. As a special gift and to help you embed the leadership skills that firefighters use everyday into your own life, I would love to give you a **FREE** copy of the audiobook.

Just scan the QR code, enter the PASSWORD and details, and I'll email you a copy.

You might also find some other special gifts there to help you to become an even more amazing leader that others will **WANT** to follow into the flames!

Cheers!

Brad

Acknowledgements

Writing this book has been an incredible journey which started as an idea in 2020 during COVID, and I couldn't have done it without the support and encouragement of so many wonderful people.

First and foremost, to my family – you are my everything. Thank you for your patience and love as I spent too many hours over many years banging away on my keyboard like a meme cat.

To my mates, the volunteers of the Rural Fire Service Queensland (RFSQ), we have stood side by side in the worst conditions and won, time and time again. I'm inspired by your strength, resilience, selflessness and your devotion to your communities and each other. You taught me how to be a leader and I'm forever grateful for your support.

To my mentors, colleagues and friends in the business world, your stories, advice and experiences have deeply enriched this book. You've taught me more than I could have ever imagined and made me more successful than I ever thought I could be..

A huge shout-out to my editor, my publisher, my friend, Dixie Carlton – your sharp eye and insightful feedback turned my rough drafts into something I'm truly proud of. Your dedication and patience have been invaluable.

To my friends who read bits and pieces of the book as I wrote them, thanks for your time, feedback and "keep goings". Your belief in me kept me going when I didn't believe in myself.

And finally, to you, the reader and the leader. Thank you for picking up this book. I hope it provides you with the insights and inspiration to lead with agility and confidence when the world around you starts to rapidly come apart. Here's to embracing change and running towards the flames together!

About the Author

Brad Hauck is a distinguished leader with a unique blend of experience as a volunteer firefighter and digital marketing expert. For over two decades, Brad has served as a volunteer firefighter in Australia, responding to numerous bushfires and mastering the art of adaptability and resilience. His firefighting journey, inspired by his Godfather, has taught him the importance of quick decision-making and calm leadership under pressure.

In parallel, Brad has built a successful career in digital marketing since 1996, specializing in search engine optimization (SEO). He has helped countless companies achieve top online rankings, navigating the ever-changing digital landscape with strategic thinking and agility. His dual careers have provided him with a profound understanding of managing change and leading effectively in unpredictable environments.

In *Run Towards the Flames* Brad shares his insights on leadership and change management, drawing from his extensive experiences in both firefighting and digital marketing. His mission is to inspire readers to confront challenges head-on and embrace change with confidence and preparedness. Brad's story is one of courage, continuous learning, and dedication, making him a compelling voice in the world of leadership.

Brad is available for keynote speaking engagements at conferences and events, where he shares his unique stories and insights on leadership, resilience, and rapid change. His dynamic presentations inspire audiences to confront challenges head-on and embrace change with confidence and preparedness.